RESISTANCE IS A BLUE SPANISH GUITAR

Poems by
George Wallace

BLUE LIGHT PRESS ◆ 1ST WORLD PUBLISHING

1st WORLD PUBLISHING

SAN FRANCISCO ◆ FAIRFIELD ◆ DELHI

Resistance Is a Blue Spanish Guitar

Blue Light Press
www.bluelightpress.com
bluelightpress@aol.com

1st World Publishing
PO Box 2211
Fairfield, IA 52556
www.1stworldpublishing.com

Book & Cover Design
Melanie Gendron
melaniegendron999@gmail.com

Cover Art
Octavio Quintanilla

Author Photo
Mark Strodl

First Edition

Library of Congress Cataloging-in-Publication Data

ISBN: 978-1-4218-3694-2

Acknowledgement

Grateful acknowledgement to the following publications, in which some of these poems have appeared: ***Bang*** (Cooling it with you in the higher elevations, Lorca doesn't drink here anymore, Dakota); ***Beat Generation Anthology 2020*** (Misunderstanding Colorado); ***Clasex Press Broadsides 2020*** (Hemingway's favorite bar); ***Conestoga Zen*** (Chelsea Piers, chapel of moonlight; Listening to jazz on a rainy bebop afternoon; So long Alabama); ***Corona*** (If only I could play Faure's Requiem like Lorna Breen); ***Covid, Isolation and Hope: Poets responding to the Pandemic*** (Ambulances are screaming down 7th Avenue again); ***Fog and Light: SF through the eyes of the poets who live here*** (A place called Stoney Creek); ***Gasconade Review*** (An ocean of grass but now it's progress); ***Hello Future*** (The future is an endless procession with horizon, Pale rider); ***Hera the light of women*** (When Ruth Bader Ginsburg stood); ***Heroin Love Songs*** (Drinking the Green Fairy, Ozone Cowboy); ***Maintenant 14*** (Bees in the orchard, butterflies in bright pairs); ***Pandemic Puzzle Poems*** (Quarantine days, Yellow moon gone pink); ***Pedestal Magazine*** (Hauling coal in paradise); ***Piccolo Museo della Poesia*** (And there will be peace at the end to the world); ***Rucksack: A Global Poetry Patchwork*** (Man, master and servant of the machine); ***Trailer Park Quarterly*** (I drove west because of you); ***Waymark*** (Little child, fisher of dreams; Resistance is a Blue Spanish Guitar, Under a tin shed in the tropical rain); ***White Rabbit*** (Rain in Cincinnati); ***Whitman Collaborative Project*** (I look to my hands and do not complain)

Contents

Lorca doesn't drink here any more

If only I could
remember your
words (horses
mountains
gypsies in
gypsy bars)
love pain
lost faith &
socialism
commingling
in the August
heat — we drank
together here
we made love
there (a man
with a blue
guitar proud
disdainful
laments all
the sensuality
of old Spain)
(at a corner table
an old man w/
silver eyes empties
mountain passes,
recites poetry) in
fact all Andalucia
was singing &
Federico Garcia
Lorca you were
singing (rural
songs sung

darkly, I cannot
remember the
words) motionless
as a lizard on a
hypnotist rock
your eyes brown
as mountains (we
drank it in deep,
the shimmering
duende) 'I remember
us in better times'
you said & fingered
your wineglass
coyly, as a girl.
As a child, 'we
wandered hand
in hand in the
olive trees, you
loved me better
then' (even in the
awful silence of
Spain's simmering
heat your voice
was fresh as
fountain water,
seduced me)
— *fuentes*
vaqueros
was never far
from your lips
Federico — I was
never like you
you were cool
& handsome
I was wild &

innocent, perhaps
you secretly admired
the peasant in me
(you offered me
figs I took them
from your hands)
you filled my mouth
with poetry — I was
poor witless &
distracted in
Spain & what
you desired is
what you received —
the adoration of
a simple man
no better than
a goatherd you
picked up in
snow-capped
mountains)
— this is a
memory
I do not
share w/
just anyone —
how I was seduced
by you Garcia
Lorca, feral,
animated,
native to
Andalucian
heat — & your
hands, two
small delicate
mortal creatures (&

the sacred hot
thrum of
your voice,
how like
cicadas
singing in
the mute
lost heat of
summer)

Hemingway's favorite bar

sloppy joes corner of duval and green
mile zero on the highway that leads to
anywhere you wish you would have went
but didn't, two go-to sisters at the end
of the bar order a drink (look they call
it 'siren on the rocks' that's a laugh) —
they are drumming on their cocktail
napkins with their nails done sharp
as a six toed cat they are eating salt
peanuts they are from wisconsin they
only have three hours to pick up men
now this is a sight worth remembering
in walks this exotic looking (now there's
a real tan, grizzled chin, that patch over
one eye is probably overkill) gentleman
plenty of free-flowing cash hell why not

looks like odysseus and his crew of shipwrecked sailors
are going to get lucky tonight

the party is on they have turned their
backs on time while outside in the key
west sky the sun is slipping on its pink
and red negligee and is taking a nose
dive into the gulf of mexico o! pay it no
mind ladies (the cat-juggler is warming
up his act the tourists are beginning to
arrive here comes the tight rope walker
in his orange cargo shorts) — it's 7:57 in
mallory square hemingway's favorite bar
is emptying out better move quick ladies
this is mile zero on the great american
highway your fantasy vacation is only
a sunset away from erasure

Rain In Cincinnati

Daylight settling, winter settling, dusklight falling rich and red, sweet as sloe, eyes heavy, a pinpoint job ready to explode, waiting for the pitch dark, not enough Denny's in a cup to fuel a drive of these proportions, you could paint a still life across this country and keep going, go right off the canvas, go on painting all the way til tomorrow

Because the wild don't quit, yet like a small child playing hide and seek in dusty overalls and raw dungarees, sometimes there is a shyness about the wild, and wisdom too, you keep your pace, I keep mine — life goes on irregardless of what we are told and I am told a lot, I keep my own council and my eye on the long mile

And I breach no scandal and I do no harm because bango whango — it comes back to bite you, don't it! — whereas on a night like this, any evening really falling across broad waters like these, love goes down easy, watchful as the wild, hep to distances and critical of every face in every roadster and highbanked cloud that plays trucks overhead

Seeding the world with gems and ice, centuries, millennia, eternities of ice! like wild birds splashing down, the soft moans of lovers lying bankside — and I see your face in every headlight, flickering to life, and in these waters, biblical, still visible at dusk, I see you rising to surfaces and my own self rising too, by this light of light, which is light dissipating

This light, which is a continent drowning, a future which has come and gone, and a lover who has disappeared without a trace.

Which is this water, glint of sun that rose in Sumeria and moon-light on the Jordan River and rain in Cincinnati.

Little child, fisher of dreams

Niñita de pescadores...duerme tranquilo encima de la duna que te levanta

Little child, fisher of dreams, caught at the border,
tossed aside, brave little child, escapee from terror
at home to terror abroad, caught in the arms of a
different brand of terror, the cold hard inhumanity
of North American government, North American
lust for money, North American adults & their
inexplicable revelry & doubling down on hate,
with their bigger fish than you to fry, little child
fished from political waters, fished from the river's
sweet going & separated from your mother,
brave child, crosser of no man's land because
no land is forbidden to a child, fisher of dreams,
little child caught between intolerance & intolerance,
tossed into a cage with only your little legs to carry
you, snagged in their net of lies and excuses,
tossed aside like excess bait on capitalism's
splintery dock, scapegoat for bandits & thieves
in San Salvador and Washington DC, pawn
to fearmongers, sneered at by politicians &
their smug minions, the smiles of privilege, the
hypocrisy of words, run to me child, you who
would escape them with your little legs, run to
me, with your enormous tears — sleep easy,
I am the dune that will lift you from this place —
you who would unbind the knots of selfishness with
your unblemished love, you who would overwhelm
The terrible power of the state with your enormous tears,

I will cradle you.

(after Canción de Pescadoras, Gabriela Mistral)

Blue Allegheny in the mist

Honey what do you want from me
if I had a gun I would shoot up a bank
withdraw ten thousand dollars pay
off the devil & buy us two tickets to
paradise (let's stop along the way
I want a green tattoo on my left
shoulder w/ dragonflies flying all
around it) but I don't have a gun &
no we are not built that way we are
neither of us made out of gun barrel
steel we are stuck in a town where
anyone's heart can turn to rust in no
time flat especially when there's no
work & the mill's shut — it's a long
hard road between this place & a
bottle of parlez vous ain't it honey
& if I had a heart I'd tell you lies & if
you had a heart you wouldn't be here
with me in the first place — O we are
a pretty pair, can't help betting on
each other & if you had a heart I'd
break it right now & if I had a heart I'd
drive you home to your old man — &
what is so strange & tender as Blue
Allegheny in the mist

(No don't answer
that question
honey things
are better
this way)

Too many catfish for one little hole

Mud in the basement kitten in the well
the only thing that ever gets me DOWN
Is you honey, the things you do to yourself
not what you do to me, it's never been

About me with you — we both know that —
but I just don't understand, who does it pay
No I don't understand and I can't stop you
from doing what the devil must've told you

You're not the only one I suppose, guess
I'm the same, guess a lot of us around here,
the same, none of us has got the power and
none of us has ever really took the cure —

And it's muddy at the bottom and there's roses
in the darkness and a dream on every hook
and freedom is a train and that's music to my
ears and it's mine for one damn second

And it's go where you got to go

Too many catfish for one little catfish hole —
maybe that's the way it's supposed to be

Maybe that's what muddy means —

Dark at the bottom, brighter on the top some day

Warhol soup

Nihilism
must've
been
nice
a side-
show for
you
once
(too many
casual
terror dates
for me,
outside
Jersey
City,
disorganized
petty crimes
committed
cheek to jowl,
pressed hard
against a
Motel 6
window
pane)
being
you were
well-hung
photogenic
& privately
endowed
in leather
boots a

precious
objet d'art
clung
like a
Ming vase
to the
back of
some
motor
cycle
assdaddy
(no mattress
for you in
Reno) but I
saw thru that
the moment I
met you in the
hospital after your
latest freak out
(never mind
what I was
doing there),
the Gulf Coast
was malarial,
outside an
ocean of
parking lots
waved like
palm trees
sick with
paradise
(full disclosure:
this image
has been
modified to

erase the
truly
walking wounded)
you lay there
like a dozen
roses in a plain
wooden box
explaining
everything to
me (including
Proust) until the
television crew from
LA arrived (that fat
producer laughing
in the hallway,
news at 8) and
you clammed
up — it was all
Warhol soup
(you showed me
your wrists I showed you
my Munch tattoo)
& that
was that,
start of it all
— being
a pair of
nineteenth c.
romantics
at heart
we under-
took a
lifelong
quest
to know

each
other
perfectly
morbidly
& well

(tr. better than
ourselves)

The Real Dookie

He wasn't a poet he was an old wooden bucket, plenty of horses had drunk from him on Manhattan island and poets are horses and he ran wild with the horses until he was sore in his ribs with all that running

"Time to bury me
with the Nag's Old
Head" he said

But he went to Oakland instead and hit the ground running it was 60's Berkeley (where else would a poet go in those bold muscular days) and he spoke out loud and the poets listened and everyone who heard his voice

Knew he was the Real Dookie slinging it at the beatnik cafe and down by Jack London's pier and his poems piled up against the pylons like sea foam and litter and he plied the liminal space between the physical and the surreal

Like a tramp steamer cutting through foul harbor waters and headed out to sea until in his raw western power he hit full throttle (he could burn whole mountains and make shit float) but then one day

'I fly them, but I'm not
in them,' he said of his poems
in a pique of inexplicable candor

And that was when they stopped listening they shadowed him out they abandoned him to his old rattling East Coast bucket of a voice — so he went home bypassing New York entirely, all the way to the old country of his ancestors,

Shepherdesses and highlanders all, where the streams and rocks were still fragile and green and the hillsides listening and the sheep coming up to smell of his blood and recognize him as one of their own and

That was the Real Dookie on a green hillside all right!

At night along with the stars listening; and in the morning the sun and morning clouds

Coming on to him like a child.

Rapture in Aisle Nine

Rapture in
aisle 9
someone
clean up
the spill
our joys
are over-
flowing
be jubilant
America
capitalism
is a pinada
smack it
in the face
(with a cop
baton) and
the donkey
explodes!
toys fall
out of the
sky like fake
diamonds
shake
down
para-
dise!
it's all
a fake
so what
the shelves
are full the
ravishment of

the people
is complete
put down yr
weapons boys
go back to
your mancaves
you have won
the day you have
held back the enemies
of corporate America
let's go down to
the courthouse

They're handing
out badges at
noon (o so lucky
O so great) (all
it takes is a big fat
lie & enuf suckers
willing to use pepper
spray) let's put up
a monument (better
put a fence around it
mr president) we
have subdued
the wild waters
of justice,
citizens,
all hail
our great
and open-
fisted leader
who has laid
his hand
on a bible

and made us
holy — spread
the news the
wealth of
our nation
is secure and
shall pour forth
from heaven
like dominoes

Now may the sun
shine bright
on this great
land of
ours!

(Rooster, call up
the sun)

A fine Cajun stewpot

In the land of the carnivalesque satire is a kind of sanity, to start; Rabelais rules the new world, the humor and excess of sexual appetite, greed incarnate sliced through like butter, while the abbot remains intractable on the subject of victuals and their correct allocation,

(They feed so well and copiously, the rich, while the villagers mete out the last of their year-end worn-out potatoes)

And by such grotesquery is the revolution forestalled, a countervail and a revelry, a one day equalizer, *Courir de Mardi Gras* a fine Cajun stewpot shared with the masses, an unctuous morass, this masque and march of sycophants, heirs of the usual medieval privations; ie France when the stores gave out the peasants went door to door demanding bread, otherwise you'd suffer the annual plague of chicken theft and pig tackling, Mardi Gras was better (and the fat louts waltzed one by one with the widow, she who was easy on the pocketbook and her lips like black cherry, she whose breath was a crypt of chalk, and her complexion the color of lilacs);

(But see how the orchestra pauses and the giddiest grow pale)

And see how — O! grotesque and opulent god — you find us now, as you would have it, gripped in the entire blindness of your perfect day; gullets lined in crimson satin, engaged in the red-letter polyglot of compensatory wealth and vulgar gyrations;

We who are clothed in royalty now, every man a king;
We who marry quick and variously, and hoard our riches;

We who boil off the fat, and drink the liquid texts of generations;

We who swallow the pork shoulder whole, without chewing, and spit out the bone.

Drinking the Green Fairy

old poets & absinthe drinkers should travel in packs I heard
wm j taylor jr the very good sf poet got rolled the other night
under a street lamp nr the vampyre boutique in NOLA (that
big bukowski conference had just broke up) he wanted to try

every absinthe in town & walked into 'a speakeasy for reals'
a couple of hours later stevie nicks was swimming thru wm
j taylor jr's head someone twisted his arm took his id & all his
money (gave him a black eye for good measure) & he had

trouble getting onto a plane the next day ('even the birds in
NOLA are friendly' sd wm but that was at ten & the sun still
shining); absinthe's a gas NOLA's crazy & people in some
towns can fool you with their friendliness — I know, I been

there myself but I'm old now & no longer drink alone after 3
am in strange towns (wonder did they take the amulet wm j
taylor had bought earlier that night 'it was for protection' he
sd 'a spell candle, those goth girls are very serious about it')

An Elegy for Steve Dalachinksy

They announced you dying during the open mic at the Parkside Lounge, Sunday the 15th of September (while the crowd in the barroom beyond the curtains cheered or fell silent on cue depending on the score, the New Orleans Saints were losing on widescreen TV), and nobody in the joint cared about football or poetry anymore, all they cared about was you (you would have hated that line and heckled me for it from the back of the room and then embraced me afterwards, kissing me on the top of my head like the brother I never had, to fight with and to love);

Steve Dalachinsky, the ethology of connectedness flowed through your veins like the tongue of G-d, latter day Apollinaire wailing like Cecil Taylor in the last days of the Great American Empire of Jazz, zone of your own, intricate, troubled, fine (I read your manuscripts, your words spilled across the page like lost tribes of Israel, no stage could hold such restless energy);

Just as I read you in all your seasons — celebrating spring at the Botanical Gardens (Yuko plucking wayward cherryblossoms from your shirtsleeve); lounging bare-chested as a lizard on a summer ledge of rock at Esopus Creek; admiring the funerary flowers of autumn, leaves ripening on trees (we drove through New Jersey on a highway overlooking the Palisades);

Or laughing with old Gerd Stern in the slush of some street corner in NYC, shuffling your feet like two charliechaplins in winter;

I imagine you standing on the pavement outside the gates of heaven — hawking readings to come on slips of paper no bigger than the size of your thumb — bitching about the price to get in;

Or just performing, performing, performing, in NYC church basements and radical worker halls, in smoky Paris and Tokyo dives, at Woodstock town hall and in Brooklyn tenements, every damn poetry club and second story walk-up you could score;

(Remember that Ira Cohen bash at Zebulon, you were cracking jokes while Ira danced on the screen, reel to reel, on the crowded banks of the Ganges);

(Or in the courtyard behind Steve Cannon's place, mosquitoes buzzing at your neck, you shoo'ed them away in the dark, the bloody night swelling with your music);

Comrade, brother, one man jazz ark-estra, fellow traveler on some arcane esoteric mission from heaven, the only grown man to ever call me Georgie, the only grown man to call me when my own heart gave out,

RIP — I never got to thank you for teaching me how to sing.

Beat Goddess: for Ruth Weiss

dragon in
the house
poetry
warrior
of the
north
beach
beanery
scene,
beat
goddess
tempered
by earth-
quake &
mendocino
mud a cabal of
one, poorly
disguised
in your
mortal
coil
street
soldier
of the
strange
American
1950s,
what
under-
ground
fog of
jazz

secludes
you now,
you! re-
making
the rules
of cool w/
your long
suffering
modesty
gem-like
among
the self-
made self-
aggrandizers
you were more
magnificent than
they (stood tall
among the
redwoods all
5 foot 2 you
climbed the
mayan pyramid)
tall as any tree
or poet northern
california ever pro-
duced (you shaved yr
head in '65, decades after
escaping europe and
the nazis) you blew
secret code
w/ America's
black rimbaud
tight-lipped
true & holy
stripped down

jazz prose
having seen
the worst of
men (you
could also
express
the most
sublime)
you! who
survived
what the
rest could
only imagine
(the killing fields of
dachau) lord
bless & protect
you still, beat
goddess, as
you leave us
for the rarefied
climes from
which your
soul came
farewell!
soaring
heaven-ward
on those
groovy
dreadful
tempered
wings

A little poem for David Olney

"the women 'cross the river carry water from the well at break of day"

Here's a glass of whiskey & an elegy for Dave Olney, whose
songs made other people famous, not him; to a man who did
not make the headliner list on January 18 2020 at a folk festival
in Florida, like Brian Wilson, Tanya Tucker, or John Prine did;

Who took the stage anyway, beautiful, 71 & obscure, who
played like he always played, obdurate fluid sweet & well, not
quite in the limelight, not quite out of it;

How he started his set, stopped, put his guitar carefully down,
apologized to the crowd, and died, still sitting on his stool (how
gently he closed his eyes; how humble the beautiful bearded
chin of his, falling to his chest);

Yes here's a glass of whiskey, sufficient to his rising & his fall;
sufficient to his final bow to the crowd; sufficient to his song,
and our imperfect knowledge of it;

Sufficient to his gaze, fixed forever on some holy place
beyond the grave, beyond audience, beyond fame, beyond the
boundaries of reputation and applause;

To a place across the river where our gazes also turn

Man, master and servant to the machine

Death came to me in the dark, with its smokestacks singing.
'Work is beautiful,' said death, 'and the machine is a woman.
Come with me through the factory gates, we will blow smoky
kisses at each other in the mysterious dark.'

'I'm taking you to a better place,' added the factory. 'A place
where you have never been.' Factory covered my eyelids with
soothing kisses.

Then in the dark how the bedsprings shook, how my head spilled
out like a river of identical hot rivets poured across the factory floor.

I took death's hand.

'The number of guys I kiss!' said death.
'The number of guys I kiss.

Well that don't matter. It's how I kiss 'em.'

Fallen Leaves

In the Kroger
parking lot
how carelessly
they fall how
effortlessly I walk
among them
amused, aroused,
falling, fallen, gone!
I stoop to pick one up,
examine it closely
(I am stubborn in my
old age) give it the
once over (what poor
flesh we have become
you and I) give it a rest
mate! I am ready for
my closeup Mister
DeMille (what a thrill
to have been your star,
dressed in autumn, for even
one glorious season) but
look at these poor veins
(that pulsed once with sap
and sun), so thin! and
I know everything must die,
children of a beautiful age,
children of an ugly age too (it's
all the same, but O how I hate you
death, my furious lover) and
these fallen leaves (how
easily they break apart
in my hands) more

dead than delicious
and I, who must taste
of them any way
I may (being neither
flesh nor fully rotted —
being godless, save for
the mysteries of flesh

I drove west because of you

I drove West because of you, and for you, heard your voice
in moonlit miles, crossed the Jesus-infested sky, caught hell
at every six-gun speedtrap and felt envy smiling at every exit
ramp; I tasted blood in a coffee cup in Abilene and in Nevada
the six month rain never came, I slept like the damned, fouled
in the yellow arroyo, and killed a horntoad with a wiper blade
because I thought I heard it say your name;

And I drove west because dry dead riverbeds spring to life
and dull horizons climb to heaven, and because the cascade
of Nebraska greengrasses is unyielding; I wept over you like
embroidery, and wanted to love you, but could not; and wanted
to understand you but could not; and wanted to rescue or
replace you, but could not;

Yellow prairie sun limp
over the statehouse dome,
your voice is like the Little Colorado,
river carving a deep ditch deeper,
out of the flesh of the virgin;

Your voice is cavernous, recalling crocodiles and thin-necked
ibis, red seas parting;
and I wanted to redeem you, but could not;

On your lips the song of endless cattle,
in your palm, spit of ancient leather,

In my rear view mirror an unregulated militia of two-bit cow-
boys shooting their fool shotgun mouths off like Washington
politicians;

And I drove west because of you

And heard your voice in full wing, like larks; your voice quick as
bullet trains kicking up wagon dust, your voice cheap as crimes
and easy encroachments;

Your voice a bone-thin man with one eye on the horizon
and the other eye missing, hell bent on death, on survival, on
oblivion;

Your voice, wet boots trampling out the vintage across this
intractable nation

Misunderstanding Colorado

Earth is the
language of
heaven like
the gods who
first fashioned it
are the language of
Men & the mountain
and no exception, gape-
mouthed as a teen,
unappeasable,
& on a short fuse
offering shelter
one day to those
lost out in it (fresh
flowing water
for the village,
running meat
for the hunt),
but also prone
to violence

(In short, mercurial, though most of all divinely indifferent to the affairs of humans)

All day in sun
wind rain etc.
standing under
a quicksilver sky
will make a mountain
inventive (ie anthropo-
morphic) designing
verbs to match its

actions, adjectives,
nouns to match its
moods ("bring me
men to match my
mountains" sd
Samuel Walter
Foss the librarian/poet,
misunderstanding
Colorado) (the year was
1894, a grotesque &
godless age of empire &
human apocalypse)

The people who worship mountains do not gut them

They listen
for the breath
of mountains
& holy new
words (shook
up words &
sanguine
that fill its
absurd mouth
to overflowing)
glorious words,
aboriginal words,
hewn by the force
that drives mountains
up out of earth's
hideous crust
(like dinosaurs,
like ants,
like birds,
like us)

& into
the thrilling
expanse of
endless
air

In the middle distance

Hub of corn, hub of wheat, hub of grain grain & tractors
& grain, glistening in the stardew, corn to feed cattle
& hogs, chemicals to feed the soil of a continent, to
renew it, sod soil root & all the lesser species bending
their necks to the will of man, nation of homesteaders,
hub in the middle distance, where hoofprint gave way

To wagon & plow, thresher & missile silo & Willa Cather
'dissolved into something complete & great' (until it was
replaced), where Jimmy killed the big snake with a spade
& became a big man, a rattlesnake so old it was left
over from before the white men came, struck him from
hate, struck him from joy, struck him across the neck &

Ended his wavy ways, like rippling fields of yellow wheat left
for dead under an endless Nebraska sky, that blossomed
with sod houses & cities, with asphalt crossing flat water
& table land under endless stars & prairie night, uncut
gems the dark flowers of regret that never betrayed their
purposes, just shone darkly on, from horizon to horizon

An ocean of grass but now it's progress

This was my America, ocean of grass, mountain of rock,
rushing volcano of lava and steam, continent of lynx and
snowrabbit and cuckoo, undisturbed land, contemplative,
conversation of waterfalls linked to each other by secret
underground caves; my America, without me in it, landing
field to raptors, fat with running birds, chest high, horses
unshod, an unsettleable land in its deep chain of sleep,
not ready to be woken to ax or plow, whip or saddle, nor
stiff-necked church, not ready for redneck bulletholes in
barrel cactus, antlers nailed to barn walls, speedtraps and
billboards among the pines, not yet, not just yet;

This was my America, before all that, mountainpeaks
fuming at each other, entrails of magma and smoke,
elk, deer, blackbear, gentle species in an ungentle land,
not ready for Columbus and rape, not ready for Andrew
Jackson and trail of tears, nor Horace Greeley and go
west young man, nor the Frenchman's rough wandering
madness, draped in wretched pelts;

Not ready for smooth-talking Reagan, Wild Bill's circus of guns;
or 35 millimeter action rifles exploding like furious candydrops
or milldams or grinding wheels or office parks or sprung mattresses
or dead rubber tires;

(In the movie version we are a beautiful but damaged nation
with a heart of gold, seeking freedom or love, Marilyn Monroe
squares her pretty shoulders, leaps out of the pickup truck,
shimmies across 50 fateful yards of Nevada desert, and stops
Clark Gable from harvesting the last of the wild horses);

This was my America, a different set of gods and god
languages, no European tongue; streams spoke to the
trout, Western Salmonback spoke to the oceans, and
empty canyons spoke like empty canyons, prairie
dogs listened to the prairie wind;

And now we are neck deep in the damage, and it is Sunday
in the rankling mire, churchbells ding like broken cups;

Plow on with your fetid swindle, America! with backhoe and
beaver trap, with combine and drone, plow on! with hands
cupped tightly to each ear, dead to anything but your own
appetite,

A volcano lived here once but now it is grazing land
an ocean of grass, but now it is progress —
nomadic tribes lived here once but now it is plunder

His love affair with the canyon

He could see the need, carved by wind, he could spread his wings to fill it, wild as life is itself, he could be a rogue canyon man, altered by circumstance yet rare as a river mink, common as greenleaf manzanita;

A water-carved western arroyo of a man, erect stem, descending root, his love affair with the canyon unfaltering, his vision primal; embryonic survivor in the throat of the plow, sad, beautiful, an isolated spire;

He could be a lone coyote loping along trails, the oldest known creature on earth at home among gambel oak and steep montane, swarmcloud in the sullen brow, rapids carving a man's bones; he could be hoofspark, one with the flash flood and the wild trout, opalescent as streams;

The pure crystal awareness of the man! tuned in by star-nativity, a scorpion, adherent to the canyon's parched terrain as a planet is to its own sweet orbit, a bearded mountain goat unobstructed by farm or marriage or concrete dam, totem with a red heart, Antares!

How unbound the swallowtail feasting by morning sun, how purposeful the bat; darting over the river by evening (the need to carve and to stay is deep, the need to flow freely, intentionally, or to die well, profound);

Creature of gravity and wind, in the upper altitudes and great basins, and in cloud forest, creature of ice and of sun, shaman of blue lightning in the gully, he could be a brushfire of a man in dry open land;

The wingspan of a man, sleeping easily among rockflower and winding scrub (how patient the desert in its bed of sand, how quick the whiptail nosing through a mountain of leaf litter);

He dreams he is a bristlecone pine, releasing large yellow pollen-clouds over the land; he dreams he is hoodoo, arch, moqui stone; he dreams he is polysymmetric, androgynous, never more loved, never more bravely;

A rock tumbling 6,000 ft. over the limestone precipice knows its own mind

Hey boys, this is a dream

Night, deep rich night, criminal with hope and rich with expectations, a little too rich for an old man dancing down Riverside Drive at 3 am in the morning but hey boys, this is a dream, the dream is a GTO and it's 1964, I am seventeen and America is a yellow rose, America is expansion and the road is empty, let's roll!

So I cut into gear and make my way, I step on it, best shot is to get moving fast before the world wakes up, grab the Henry Hudson and head north, bull my way into the passing lane slip across the bridge and head for Albany, we could make Albany by dawn, wheel left and then it's straight as piss, 3000 miles to San Francisco, O hell yeah, easy

So I gripped the wheel and I stepped on the gas (core metaphor for raw immense American power)

But the joke was on me, I got the metaphor wrong, the pedal was an egg and the egg shell broke and the engine of American commerce was a fake, all billboards and false advertising — yolk all over my shoes, cars vans breadtrucks cross-country rigs everyone flying every which everywhere a million miles per hour except me, I was broke down in the passing lane with fists shaking, the windshield a maze of glass, headlights splintering my eyes;

And I was not seventeen I was awash in capitalist elbows and get-the-hell out-of-the-way old-man trash talk and irate expressions —

It must be dawn, it must be dawn, I cried!
and it was dawn; casual dawn on Riverside Drive,
and all across America, Kennedy was dead, the dream was over

So here's a yellow rose that will not open
with ashes for eyes, of course
gateway to America and world hegemony

Ozone Cowboy

Road warrior, car jack, sunset pilot
snarling, snarling, snarled, air too thick
for the passing lane, life around here's
a joke, fuck this town been stuck
in the wrong lane since yesterday
& I'm late for the ozone festival,
I'm a gasaholic shoot em up patriot I'm a
sunsick cowboy caught in the nightmare corona
& this is a warzone baby LA's crazy,
ain't that a shame this is not why we came here,
what's the use what's done is done, nauseous!
I have took so much sun in by the mouth
my lungs don't work at all I'm Godzilla now,
this is the language of a million dinosaur years,
a helicopter is cruising the Pacific Rim,
police cars falling out of the sky like fat raindrops,
I swat 'em out of the air for fun,
they can't see me in my shades,
I'm cool man, I am an amoral reptile
put your weapons down officer
untwist your tail I will cut off your head
& get away fast, so what I'm a sparkplug
in the human ocean, I am a piston busting
crankshaft (do you talk the highway talk?)
I believe I have rode this way forever

Bull Rider in the rodeo sky

Bull Rider
in the
rodeo
sky
kicking
up
dust
like
breadloaf
clouds
sweating
in the
chute
(is that
the sun
or is it the
meanest
line of spit
ever to
fall from
a bull's
crazy
mouth)
I knew
where you
was headed
when you hit
13 a skinny kid
but up for any brand
of trouble you
could find &
okay we had

that fight
you & me
& then you
just up &
took off,
shot out
the gate —
yr mother
blamed
me — but
I never
gave up
on you
& sure
enough
one day
we seen it —
yr name on the
rodeo poster —
so we come to
look at you in
the chute
taking it
easy
drawing
a draw from
a whiskey
flask — yr
making yr
living 8
seconds
at a time
all right
& I gotta
say it looks

good on you
— majestic
w/ yr rough
manners &
the flint in
yr eyes it
looks like
you come up
roses (lucky like
yr dad pulling
carnations
out of yr
cowboy
ass) well
son if it
suits you
it suits me,
by god we
love you
no matter
what just
hang on
for dear
life & I'll
catch up
w/ you after
it's all over
at the mile-high
roundup hell
we'll go
another
round —
the 2
sweetest
cowboys

(this side
of Abilene)
anybody's
ever seen

Somewhere south of Mojave crossing

Standing outside the
only open honkytonk
in town Miller Lite
neon sign blazing
this vision of eternity
night blind grim rider
past hundred miles you
felt like your guts'd
explode, only the
moon for company
racing along like a
faithful old hound —
overhead thousands
of stars staggering
drunk as rodeo clowns,
angels doing wheelies in
the pure black chalkboard
sky, yeah we have all seen
acrobats back home
and straightliners but
nothing like this, wild
dogs in the irrigation
ditch, hoot owl splicing
the high beams, big barrel
cactus imitating movie
desperados — yeah
you seein' it all, boy,
Guthrie's ribbon of
highway so thin
you could truly piss
through it, wondrous
illogical dream road,

rules you couldn't
possibly understand,
what is this power
you possess to
drive a man mad
and just keep driving
til he's drove out,
strung out, thirsty eyed,
blind bladder, busting
all the sad beautiful
beatitudes, making all
the wrong moves —
menus, directions,
drug cocktails, worn
out prescriptions, a
million million miles of
road ahead, dipping along
like the finger of god in a
deep inkwell of silvermoon —
effluence of the divine —
and a man's got to pull over
sometime, son, somewhere
between nowhere and nowhere,
it don't matter, on the edge
of a town, at a blinking light,
no matter how hard you want
to keep on rolling to the big
light at the end of the world,
call it Vegas call it Flagstaff if
you want — light is only a myth —
dawn will always be a hundred
miles east of wherever it is you
find yourself — and maybe this
honkytonk will let you in and
leave you the hell alone, all

you've got to your name is a
few cigarettes and the dust in
your lungs, maybe a quarter
or two stuck to your ass, you
could play a song on the juke
with that, otherwise you're
busted! you are a ghost
who saw a ghost and ran,
an ordinary time-traveling
empty-headed cowboy
without a heart — look at
those boots, where you from,
LA? that haircut, those eyes —
you got nothing to hustle, no
point even trying to roll you
in the parking lot, turn you
upside down and see what
shakes out — nothing! —
nobody's gonna give you
a second look in this town
or the time of day — only the
cop in the patrol car, rotating
around the corner at 5 miles per,
with his blue lights flashing

Dakota

Leaning SSW into the
colossal darkness that
comes before dawn,
listening for the holy
drone of civilizations,
short-lived, transient,
and the voices of gods
that drove them across
this land, America, I am
driven too, I drove the
golden spike, I tapped
the underground spring,
I unleashed iron and oil,
diamonds & coal, I fired
the miner and hired the
cook, I am nobody put
up to no good, raise no
statue to me; and yet I
am somebody, with my
painterly eyes and my
ribs like ambition, my
reason quick as ponies,
my intuition native to
every land that calls
me home, attuned to
natural rhythms, I am
all ears like drums, I am
all sweat lodge, reverent;
i am no regret and tall tales
told by the campfire, you will
find me soon enough if you
dig deep enough and are patient,

I am clumsy as bear scat
and also the turtle's egg;
I am the wild orphan child,
an Irish coracle abandoned
to the reeds, returned to silkie;
I tie rattles around my ankles
when I dance like bones; and
when I sweat I sweat ginger root,
and when I am curious, then
I am my mother's child again,
innocent in her arms; and I
am of the sweet-grass, yes
you can smoke me if you
want to, and the stone pipe,
that's me too and there's
plenty more of me where
that came from, O I am mad,
mad as Blake, Ginsberg taught
me how to chant this song and so
did my good gray Uncle Walt; O
read my eyes America I am
talking to you, like Kansas
leafhoppers spoke to Kerouac;
I am a cradle left out in a squall,
I am rocking; the summer rain
which cools you cools me too,
and the lightning which spooks
horses spooks me; and yes,

I am an offering, I am full of tobacco, disoriented, buzzing like flowers, aromatic; a pouch passed hand to hand, w/ shavings of red cedar, that's me; toss me aside for empty when you are done with me, the less of me that is left the more I become;

I am smoke, disappearing,
returning, like the curvature

of the sea that once swept this
horizon, so I too remain calm,
all surface, a full moon gliding
across my face is something
like peace (my guts swimming
w/ eels) and I am erasing my
own footprints as I cross sand;
(what is this thing
called sand, I
am wind I am rock
I am sand)
and I am like tombstones and
monuments, I keep myself busy
(as if this poem were
eternal! as if you,
reading this poem,
were eternal!)

No more presidents no more
wars; no more statues no more
flags. No more governments!
only this: lakes, rivers, holy, original;
prairies, introverted and shy;
foxes, laughing and goofing
along as they go;

To be stuck here, one more day,
irreverent! With you, an old man
not quite monk, painted on a scroll,
one foot in heaven and the other
in the shitter, with a jug of wine
in your arms & a shack of wind
for shelter

Leaning out through the enormous window to take a piss before the cold weather comes.

A place called Stoney Creek

Here in the city
people take care
of themselves
on the farm
(where you
grew up) every
thing takes care
of everything else.
cows take care of
horses, horses take
care of men, men
take care of barns &
plows & tractor engine
parts take care of each other.
bees take care of clover & clover
takes care of bees (who are also taken
care of by beekeepers) & the fields are
alive with California Poppies that wobble in
the orange-yellow breeze. I don't know
how these things work, I am just a man
of the city I'm lucky if I can take care of
myself one day to the next. But I try
best as I can & I leave the rest to
chance & dream that we don't
live here in the city at all, you &
me — we live up the coast in a
place called Stoney Creek,
Del Norte County, California,
we have milk goats & chickens
& bees we have strong children
we teach them right & we send them
on their way we have eggs & cheese

butter & milk we've got ducks in a
duck pond, an old fishing boat with
a leak in the hull, & in summer there's
long grass for mowing & in spring
there's short grass for making love in,
under the yellow California sun (yellow
of marigolds, yellow of your hair) &
sometimes you admit it, you had a
boyfriend back in the day, a farm boy
(even now when you braid your hair
with wildflowers you sing songs
you learned from him) & I skin
my knuckles on spark plugs
& chromium steel & do not
mind & often in the morning
I stop to smile because you've
made some little present for
me, with your perfectly strong
hands, left it on the kitchen counter.
This is my dream, I do not wish
to ever be free of it in fact I had
it just the other night, my dream,
you & me we drove up the coast
to the Oregon border, we left SF
way before dawn, by the time we
hit Stoney Creek it was morning,
the fields were cool with Pacific fog —
& all the way there you sang songs
that farm boy taught you and all the
way there I fell in love with you, over
and over again — because that's what I
do in my dream about Stoney Creek.
I fall in love with you — like the first
love, like the first spring. Like any
ordinary old man from the city would

do. Because I know what love is. Love
is a field of tall yellow grass with orange-
yellow poppies waving their fool heads off
in the Pacific ocean breeze. Love is clover
for bees, bees for clover.

Love is a place called Stoney Creek — and you,
braiding those long strings of wildflowers in your golden hair.

Something simple like coyotes

Sometimes when weariness gets ahold
inside this little house and the world goes
drowsy and domesticated and I am not
sure if it's me drifting off to sleep or it's
the room that is sleeping and I am wide
awake both eyes and a hoot owl's calling —
it could be the unexpected smell of rain
or something simple like coyotes or walnut
branches knocking at my window, or else
the wind kicking up or the dogs growling;
something small, anything to get my brain
going inside my head and get some big idea
— like why not go outside and have a smoke
by the corral and watch the moon come up
high over the cattle (the redfaced moon,
which rolls in late with plenty of excuses
this time of year, and anyhow only stopped
to take a piss at the gate for one little minute
before coming in)

Goodbye Angelina

Goodbye Angelina
this thing of ours
has gotten way
out of hand I'm off
to Texas and the
border this house
of yours was all
right for awhile
I suppose but
this kind of life
don't suit me &
is a metaphor
for dying one
day at a time
& anyhow we
both know your
husband will be
back from South
Dakota soon & he's
a good man too
better than me if
I remember him
right from college
a captain in the Air
Force & when his tour
of duty's done he'll be
repopulating your meta-
phorical petunias so to speak
so yes I got to move on
even if you are all
the woman I will
ever love not to be

romantic about it but
it's nearly morning
there's a state line to
cross and a long road
ahead of me — yes we
both know that you loved
me good too good maybe
better than I deserved
but I pulled my load
didn't I if you don't
count the drinking
anyhow there's no
point measuring things
love has got no calculations
no I'll just point my nose
towards Texas & be on
my way Angelina the
border is where I'm
from & headed for it's
a metaphor for freedom
& I'm a freedomloving man
so wipe away your pretty tears
I'm headed for McAllen I know
a gal there who owns a
Washateria goodbye

Zoom crash sparkle bang boom

Zoom
crash
sparkle
bang
Fourth of
July in
America
again
tripping
down fire-
cracker
lane on our
statuesque
oath-busting
oafish feet
trampling
everything
we see
prairies
seas
river-
branches
cattle-
ranches
farms
families
arbors
wilds
herds of
buffalo
and
whole

nations
of civilized
living beings
(O muddy
these pristine
waters O
drill for
oil in the
holy shale) O
cherish
this day
our great
and glorious
nation home
of victory
hoo-raw!
followers of
the biggest
baddest best
laid plan of man
(never did quite draw
a proper bead on
that one boys)
losing our way
again and
again only
to find it (only
to lose it) —
on the best
of days a well
intentioned
child-like
people
(forgive us!)
a contrite

people
who really
only wanted
to pet the rabbit
(ty John Stein-
beck) and
love the land
(O cataclysmic
joy O glimmer
O clang)

Here's a salute the humanity yet shining in our two-fisted sun-blackened deep blue gunpowder eyes

ZOOM
CRASH
SPARKLE
BANG

BOOM!

1912

Knees up
in the iron
tub I am
all of 13
    slippery as
nipples
& up to
my ears
with shame
  (all legs
in a bridal
  veil of
soap
  suds)
how to
explain
this un-
dying
affection
for my
cousin
Rebekkah
  who lives on
a small farm
  with three cats
& a chicken house
somewhere
  outside
Schenectady

Walkin' the dog

the devil
came up to
me in the
last days of
the best little
democracy that
never was
& me
walking
along
under
god's blue
heaven
w/ my
innocent
dog Sammy
thinking about
elephants
jumping
the fence
& wondering
what will save us
from ourselves
this time

maybe we really done it this time I said to the devil & he said
what?

broke the
needle
I said, maybe
we broke

the needle
for real this time
(like in that Rufus
Jackson song)
& now we won't
be able to
sew no more

the devil he just smiled
you make me laugh
he sd don't worry
about none of that
I taught Rufus that song

so I said to the devil hey man is any of this shit real?

yes
George
the devil
replied of
course
all of it
is real

how about I give you fifteen cents & you let me walk that dog
of yours awhile

so I let him

Love, in the eyes of a galloping horse

Night was black and she was in love,
she who did not know what love is or
with who, she who covered her bed in
flowers and went with it, she'd seen this
thing done -- in a movie, she just wanted
something beautiful to fill her head with,
to make her eternal, to make her as good
as love is good, because sometimes when
she closed her eye someone came to her
and told her things she didn't want to hear,
and she didn't like what she heard, no! she
wanted love, love, she deserved love, she
had seen love done in a movie, she had
heard love done in a song, she liked that,
why even her mother had once sang her
a song about love, Selena sang her a song
about love, too, and she believed in Selena
and she believed in her mother and I don't
care if Selena is dead, love is alive, eternal!
magic! And she believed in love and had
so many lovers to prove it, beautiful men,
beautiful women, girls boys men, especially
girls weeping, men gnashing their teeth,
boys cursing, jealous people everywhere
whisper they tell little lies behind her back

Who cares, this poem isn't about them

It's about love, the color of gold, which
sleeps in the deep heart of the sun
or in the eyes of a galloping horse
love galloping over sand, love, and

she knelt by her bed and wept for it
so long she ascended into the sky
where she is one of the stars,
no more, no less, twinkling

Carnalismo

Good men good women find honest work in terrible times like these here pretty bad at the moment a society best held at arm's length or walked away from like a rotten cheese —

Bad times call for strong measures like resistance like fraternity — like let loose the carnalismo baby and the best course of action sometimes is to forge our own path, together,

By the measure of our own stride
By the destiny of our own hands

  our arms are
     powerful, our legs
  strong, people!

We are the cardinal points of our own material existence.

Not exactly Spanish but something more native to this valley

In a land of pastures and the animals that graze upon them, in a land of barn and beanfield and grandmother's chickens, in a land of seed told out by the handful by women in aprons, and young men in the vicinity who will come by when you need them to help lift a heavy load;

In a land of modest reward for husband and wife, and animals that work in teams; in a land of many generations gone and more to come, and the astonishing face of Our Lady of Guadalupe which smiles down on everybody; it is new years, it is winter, and winter is the season for the virgin to smile with a deep and boundless sorrow;

Especially upon a young girl with braids in her hair and a strong disposition, an imaginative girl, musical in speech, who sings to animals in the farmyard, not exactly in Spanish but something more native to this valley;

a young girl raised like the rest but somehow she is a stranger to them, obedient to surfaces but you can see it in her eye she is faithful to a voice she alone seems to hear, sometimes she walks down the slope to the edge of the farm, where she sings songs of longing and loss to the frozen stream;

and it is winter and it is the season for gossip and for dreams, and perhaps it is that look in her eye, the light in it; perhaps it is the way she holds court among the animals (even the donkey listens) or sings to streams, 'that one's a dreamer' they say;

Because there is just something not quite right about that girl and unlike the rest of them;

And they used to talk about the old man, her grandfather, like that too; he had that look about him and practically lived outside and often slept in the stables, not an ounce of sense in his head and he refused to come inside when he was called,

And okay he managed the place well enough in his day but he had his secrets, too, and kept them to himself — which is not how things are done — what kind of a man is it who does not share everything he knows about the land, except a man who is strange, among strangers;

And now it is winter, the season of slow-passages, it is New Years, and there are these songs to be sung, not exactly in Spanish but something more native to this valley;

These songs of winter, which is the season of gossip to some and dreams to others, the season of secrets told and untold; the season when the sun stops beckoning and the animals shift heavy in the stable, beneath the astonishing face of Our Lady of Guadalupe, smiling;

And everyone in the valley waiting, as patiently as they can, for spring.

Leon Trotsky in Mexico City

Greener than
green waters
Mexico City in
the morning
the shadow
of Trotsky's
brown eyes
piercing
the courtyard
(odor of dogshit,
breath of carnivorous
summer flowers)
outside the family
compound, streetcars
are rumbling already
— Trotsky slips like
trembling water
among the agave
plants, his two
strong hands
green as angel
wings (idle at
his side he holds
a cutting
knife)
    he has finished slicing fresh pear to feed to parakeets
'*patience is more*
dangerous than
revolution'
he says,
reaching
delicately

into the wooden
cages, separating
blue birds from the yellow,
his nightshirt wet with dew,
his olive skin & shallow
breath glimmering
(why did she
marry him?
what sexual
allure did she
apprehend
beneath his
oratorical
power?) an
inner sea
rolls steady
in his blood, this
countenance of his
pure as obsidian,
sharper than
Spanish steel,
resolute as
an Aztec as he
parts the waters
of the material
world (O greener
than green the waters
that live below
the streets of
Mexico City!)

Humble as seafoam, more precious than jade

Ode to Pablo da Rokha

Gambling with the devil is a sucker's game unless you are playing with house money ie stealing language from the enemy and using it against him in which case it is all for play it is all for love and then O the game! You cannot lose Pablo da Rokha because of the shape of the fruit you eat because of the language you use it is hot it is luscious it is abundant and various it is twined like the cordillera

The living language of the Incas ripens in your mouth South American Spanish sails between your teeth, like spirits moving into and out of the world, like soil or mist, through every amalgamation of sound, soaring with the offbeat condor, your words undisciplined, wild, delicious to the tongue

You play poker with the children of the sky, you feud with Neruda or make love to your wife, you losing always losing but coming out on top, counting your losses counting your gains no money changes hands you give away no secrets your poems belch volcanoes of Marxism and smoke and reach deep into the extreme heart of the world for more

It is the language of the people and on their behalf Pablo da Rokha, your belly a dancing Titicaca of flatheaded fish, your breath extraterrestrial, swimming the Andes, your lungs a gift to the world ticking off symbols and signs like Inca rope

And your hands Pablo your hands dipping into the surface of the new world, hemisphere made good again, made rich, two hands wide as continents, a broad Canadian mist shimmers in blue summer ice, the lake of the world beams enormous laces of sundrenched light over the Bolivian plains

Not a cloud in the sky it is 1952 kilometers to Santiago you are everywhere leaping mountaintops, a waterfall transfixes the sun, a bird of prey beckons young Ernesto who pushes his Yanqui motorbike over a cliff and sings goddam! Wheezing barefooted and free 'cross the backbone of the Americas

Your lumberjack stride, your arms like all the rivers of Uruguay combined, your heartbeat like Argentine bread and voice thunderous, bespectacled beside the cool Pacific, your silver grace a pre-Colombian dawn, your consonants and vowels sacred in the midst of the 20th century melee, awakening revolutionary dreams among the people

Who has been conquered by the sword and helmet not us! O indigenous heart, *vinceremos* Pablo da Rokha, the free new world salutes you and your onslaught, via the enemy's own words, via every available language, upon oppression

O new world poet; O liberation thief; O sharp dagger into the vocabulary of the colonial treasure vault, sing! Walt Whitman de la Sud, towering masterful poet of continents! we lift our voices too and sing with you

Against the endless suffering of the people

Against the armaments of European pride

Against the contours of the Conquistador's corrosive hand

Elegy for a small rainforest

beneath the street sign, *pianos e musicas*, I see them walking, dead soldiers of the day, wheeling to the left and to the right, you know the kind, strolling deep as deep in the ennui of appetite, the nouveau riche motoring past, the poor waking late, after an all-night Brazilian *baila* funk party;

all under the shadow of mt corcovado, on their way to someplace better or worse or never mind, the ruins of the coffee age, weaker than paradise, progress stalled in the high fever pitch of 21rst century neo-fascism, these petty exhaustions, pale blue residences and gringo no-go zones, brakelights, brakelights, brakelights;

the beasts of the age, cattleranchers and cheap beef, these cruelties and desires, these violations — old greed made new, and corruption, this thirsting for profit at the feet of Christ the Redeemer, now in the shriek of grinding gears and the low muttering ingratitudes, a waiter counting out change with his long fingers and delicate hands;

suspicious glances and white upon white, all on the *avenida rio branco*, tablecloths, sunscreen, well-heeled Europeans and hustlers eager for any small victory in the mid-afternoon haze, tiled rooftops gleaming red in the hot muddle, a century of migration and exploitation and drought, no advantage too small, no triviality too obscene;

and sunlight on the scalloped bay, eternal!

see how they come, relentless as bayonets
see how they come, with drillbits and thirst for money
how they prick the sky, ravenous as children

how like match flames they would burn the earth down to its bare soil for a moment's gain;

into the dustbin, soldiers of capitalism! let us build us a city out of the bones of your ruined paradise, let us take the long drive out from here, great against the gray, into the miracle biosphere, steady on, steady on, loyal and obedient to life's higher virtues, no longer prisoners of the banal, singing sweetly a *sertanejo* song, the sweeping harmonious song of humanity;

no longer to cry for the jungle bird, or the green anaconda; no longer to cry for a small rainforest burning all day,

like the lungs of a great god burning
like smoke through sunlight, burning
like trout through rotted waves, burning

like the sham angels of progress, dead soldiers of the day, leaping with fiery wing out of the smouldering river.

Rilke's Dragon

These days
have not been
the kindest,
  there's trouble
in the land
the restlessness
has returned
   and the despair
which comes
  when women and men
    are deprived by
      fate or government
    of what it was
  made them feel
joyful in their nation
confident in their selves
(having lived
  so well
so long) hope
has been
stripped
from them
(how soon
how plum soon
they have forgot
life is not easy
people, nor
was it meant
to be) our trials are
  our proofs and
how we face them
  testament

to how great
how beautiful
  we were or
    ever could be.
Therefore welcome
great sadnesses
embrace the dark days —
what we make
of them (not
  our otherwise
meaningless lives)
are our history. Now
  have courage, have
    grace. This is the time
  the gods have given us
to reveal their presence
inside us (for the gods
do not exist except
in the manner
by which
we live
  our lives —
we are the proof
  and the substance
    of their existence).
So rip away the mask
of fear, people!
    move toward danger
  as you would opportunity,
with caution, but fearlessly —
and tackle what's left
of the great troubles
  standing tall before you
like Rilke's dragon

The Kiss

could've been
anything, even
the soul of a bird,
it landed so
surprisingly on
my parted lips —
not what I expected,
a miracle,
I guess,
so weightless
so familiar —
'un sostantivo femminile' —
having been raised
(a twig of a boy
in a great northern forest),
prim as a piccolo
& as unyielding —
unready for the
consequences —
enormous distances,
a pilgrim's progress
across wastelands
(fierce jungle heat,
alpine scrittura
of bluebells & snow) —
the glissando of
the tiniest heart,
bearing an impossible load.

The future is an endless horizon of pears

do not
ask the
piano
player
seated
alone
in a dark
corner of
le chat noir
(when it's
closing time,
the last customer
done & gone)
for a song
about the
future.
'for
every man,
in every age,
the future
dies far too
young,' he will
tell you (returning
in silence to
his cognac &
dying cigarette)
failing to
mention
that it is
also rein-
carnated
in the form
of a pear

Bertrand's teapots

how naive the
meadowlark
how artless
the song
(Ravel's
incessant
arpeggio
arcs like
this: water
music in the
fading sun) o!
that I could hold
this note for you
forever — this song
that only larks may sing —
(for you this song,
these beating wings) —
Bertrand's perfect
English teapots
rising supernaturally
toward heaven
over the sandy heath
in mid-October

Tear Down The Nazi Flag, Manolis!

for Manolis Glezos (9 Sep 1922 - 30 Mar 2020)

This urgency, this verisimilitude, this translation of the green force into utterable flesh, May 30 1941 two freedom fighters of Greece make their play, celestial firecrackers are back in business, shuffle off the mortal coil, Manolis the resurrector's back in town, the provender of chow rules, O look out Nazis! Manolis Glezos of Naxos, went to bed a slave and has woke up half man-half goat, ready to bust down your filthy larder, ready to claim your rotten vintage and your stores, you are not secure around here;

O! sweet ka-ching, tumblers fail the safe door swings wide open, Manolis (w/ Apostolis Santas) has climbed the Acropolis and torn the flag down, life and death have spoke to each other plain; and O how close the marrow of a man is to freedom (ie perpetual loins that move when new buds form) if he will only take action, how ecstatic, seedlings breaking soil in dark cellarage, bunkerflowers starving for the sun (my forehead smeared with excrement and rue);

In every bone and tongue in every arterial root the old gods dwell, waiting to be stirred awake; resistance and rebellion and underground streams flood the body of the woken few;

(I am the winnowing, the warhorse,
I am agriólykos, the wild wolf,
I am not a man — I am wanton,
I am Manolis Glezos!)

Find me in the mountain flower —
find me basking in the weeping meadow

This is my breath my body, hear me roar — I am throatwide, manfoolish, chestbare! I am the bowels, baby! I've just been disgorged from yonder crevice there!

(On 30 May 1941 Manolis Glezos and Apostolos Santas climbed the Acropolis and tore down the swastika, which had been flying there since 27 April 1941, when Nazi forces had entered Athens. This action inspired not only the Greeks, but all subject people, to resist the occupation, and established them as international anti-Nazi heroes)

Peace is honey

Peace isn't the absence of war.
It is sweet milk in a clean bucket.
It is the bleating of goats in an honest
man's yard. Peace is the honking of geese
in the pond, cicadas chirping in the tall grass.
Peace is olive presses, wine presses,
harvesters clamoring for more fruit
in the foothills of the Lower Galilee.
More than silence of dawn with no rockets
to disturb it, peace is rooster crowing,
hen clucking — plow points, shovels and
stiff rakes and hoes rattling in the back
of a pickup truck. It is the buzz of harvest
machines combing the harmonious land —
horizon to horizon, feeding all the
children women and men without
prejudice, giving all the people
in the land full employ.
Peace is Palestinian boys
in the apiaries of Doura,
west of Hebron, working
their father's hives.It is
a cloud of honeybees
hovering over the roof-
tops of Kibbutz
Ayelet Hashahar.
Peace is not just
the absence of
small arms fire,
or treaty-signing
ceremonies in
far away capitals.

It is more than just
who gets what,
who loses what,
and both sides
agree to accept it.
Peace is more than
the absence of war.

Peace is wild ducks splashing in the Jordan River.
Peace is the shared laughter of workers in the field.

Peace is honey and milk in the land of milk and honey.

Why are the refugee children smiling

The children you cage
behind bars & walls &
razor wire they are not
afraid of you — in fact
they are smiling —
in every refugee camp
In every detention center
you try to hold them in
even as you count them captive, even as you punish them for your own sins, even as you parade them before your cameras & lash them with the tongues of your ministers of hate
they see through your weaknesses
they see through your fears
they see through your crudeness & cruelty
& the futility of your old world scapegoat ideologies
in fact they see through your walls
What do they see?
they see a future
without you in it
& that's why
the refugee children
are smiling

Pale rider

Breathless as a humidor he wakes
to dawn; like a reluctant undertaker,
stiff, strung tight as a harpsichord,
contemplating his future and his past;
    (in a past life he was a captain's mate
in a pastlife he was a barber's son)

O these desolate shores! after a long
night prowling the streets of Sao Paolo
he is sore to the bone;
    in a past life he was a student in a new starched shirt

in a past life he was
a planet, molten, flung
like fire from the
belly of a star

(*You make
me smile*
he confides —
*ordinarily
I confide
in nobody*)

In a past life he was a pampas jaguar with dancing eyes

In a past life he was a shuddering dog sitting on cold clay wagging his sorry tail and watching an old hag make chimichurri for the big village fiesta

In a future life he will burn fast, like French cigarettes

Stripped of his wig and mascara, stripped of his strut and his cool calculations, he is a child really, a young boy with a future wider than the entire South American plain.

Under a tin shed in the tropical rain

they took your children from their mother's arms,
& wrapped them up in sheets of cold concrete.
they took the bread from your children's mouths
& fed it to the crows along the potomac for spite.
they took the sweat from your children's necks
they took the vision from your children's eyes.
they took your children's muscle & backbone &
they put them to work in their serious gardens.
for cocaine, for rice, for cotton oil, cane sugar.
for apples on their trees, salad on their plates.
lettuce fields! tomatoes, cabbages, yellow corn!
such pretty roses in the gardens of america!
they harvested the tears of your children, yellow
as all the tears of all the poor lying on all the floors
of the world, out of the reach of the sun, captives
in every prison and slave quarter of colonial history.
they replaced your children's sex with their filthy lies.
& the seed from your children's loins, they took
that too, spread it for fertilizer in their pulling fields.
they took the fingers from your children's hands,
wrapped them up in clear tight plastic for market.
they took the breath from your children's lungs,
the innocence from your children's dreams &
then they auctioned off the rest of your children's
bodies under a tin shed in the tropical rain.

Cooling it with you in the higher elevations

what love for the people is, two Yanquis in a jeep, crossing the Urubamba like wannabe Che and the ghost of Simon Bolivar, me in my terrible excess of residual proletariat pride, raised on grandmother's onion soup & potatoes

a pretty pair of petit-revolutionaries are we, Norte-Americanos crisscrossing the Andes with a gun-running Aussie in aviator glasses, cooling it in the higher elevations, testing the elasticity of politics against capitalist market realities

(easier to love the people when they are exotic, you said, not from our own sad lacklustre town — especially when you can turn a huge damn profit)

our devotion to the internationale is cold and durable as cold worked steel, quarreling in the marketplace over the price of freedom and fish

you with your sun hat and machete tongue, slashing big holes in the local language, me with my halting Spanish and general awkwardness of conversation among strangers (inherited from laconic peasants who made it across the Atlantic without saying a single damn word so why start now)

and carrying worn-out European manifestos

and traveled west until the west ran out (their big silent eyes and narrow ambitions)

so this is love! we're chasing long gone dreams, hauling weapons to someone else's Revolution

our love for the people is cartridges, semi-automatics

and grenade launchers packed in crates of coca cola

A White Bird with curious hostile eyes

last night in a dream I wrote in the wind
how a poem with wings nested in your heart
& sang eternal songs of spring
in the dark rooms we held each other
captive in, back in the day — you
were mercurial, impossible to hold down,
I was difficult to please, no one believed
we were possible only you and me,
nobody got hurt for very long
& our days sang like a bird in a brass cage
remembering the day it was captured
in the green hills above matagalpa
where the coffee beans grow;

a white bird with curious, hostile eyes
& we drank late into the night
& in the morning the streets were
clean & quiet, we walked to the park
& sat by the window catching
the last of the morning sun,
I read you poems by Ruben Dario
you were amused with my imperfect Spanish
& sipped your coffee, I remember eating
sliced pears & tangerines, laid out mathematically
bare on your mother's silver tray
(a gift, a magic geometry, an augury
of hope, she believed in magic
more than men, having experienced both);

our world was three rooms small, limitless in horizon,
the walls of our world solid as a penitentiary,
as a sunk keg of castilian wine,

as the hull of a wooden ship
putting out to sea in a squall

(these days are more bitter than that,
the darker days have come,
we no longer mention how delicately
we loved each other then, how we told each other
pretty lies, only, more careful
with each other's hearts)

Resistance is a blue spanish guitar played at midnight

resistance is a blue Spanish guitar played through curtained windows after midnight while the young people smoke unfiltered cigarettes in the dark and the old men avoid each other's eyes; it is the scent of jasmine, an infiltration; a pool of urine someone left in the alleyway beneath the window of the captain of the guard, as a word to the wise;

read the graffiti, boss, one day when one of your cops bends over to pick up a penny, someone will kick him in the ass — uprising, mutiny, rebellion, revolt; the overthrow of the oligarchs, discord long overdue; the lone drunk stumbling, ready for action, reckless as an onion; a half a million in the street, pulling up cobblestones;

resistance is the day of reckoning for tycoons and overlords; resistance is a calligraphy of grievances, spelled out with fists fresh on walls, this testament to the journalist who was disappeared, this testament to the hotel maid who was taken against her will; and the crooked judge in the poisonous heart of the spider web, and the government employee in his black maze of rules;

it is testament to the bloody matte of a man's skull cracked again and again until it can break no more; and billyclubbed and flattened and busted again and again, how long will a people allow injustice to declare itself so openly by name;

and I long for the day the generals wearing young girls' petticoats under their uniforms are stripped of their power and their fetishes revealed; when the rotten toadies and bigshots and aides de camp are sent scurrying from their places in the parade; when el presidente, with his pride and his strutting, is meted out his pay;

I long for the day when the bought politicians go to the window and see the resistance coming up the street with their own two eyes, and their fortifications up in smoke; for the day they piss yellow cataracts of fear into their political pants, their hypocrisy revealed as wet stains;

and injustice is a stolen egg plucked out of warm straw and given to the children of the mighty and nobody to stop it from happening, and nobody to complain; and resistance is taking the stolen egg and giving it back to the hen, resistance is power restored to the people;

and I long for the day the yolk spills out! revolution in the streets, flowing freely under the rising sun, ocean rising, golden! and the people singing their resistance song out loud; waking the spirit of freedom in the people — free like flags, free like sunlight;

free as the chords of a blue Spanish guitar played at midnight through secret curtains

An American experience

Forget the Depression, darling
try standing in front of a line
of 21rst century riot police
in your birthday suit
carrying a white envelope
full of glitterhearts & stars
chanting Black Lives Matter
under a torn umbrella

So Long Alabama

For Hank Aaron

755 blows against the Empire of Hate
755 blows against the jaw of racism
755 uppercuts and right crosses, every home run a knock out punch, 25 or more a year for 20 years in his prime

And death threats every hour of the night when he began to close in on the Babe's immortal 714

755 colossal blows against intolerance and Jim Crow and We Wash for White People Only
And step off the curb boy, keep your eyes to your damn self
755 body blows into the belly of the beast, a justice system of easy executions, not much more than an even swap for mob lynchings
755 baseballs flying over outfield walls and into the faces in the crowd; in Milwaukee and Pittsburgh and Philly and Chicago; in St. Louis; in Cincinnati and New York and Atlanta and eventually LA

310 pitchers in 31 ballparks, home runs by the fist full, great towering blasts and line drives and cheap shots that just made it over the fence, 755 of them

(Jackie Robinson had gotten there first, and Hank heard him give a talk in Mobile;
(And Hank took up the game at age 15, played for $10 per day for the Mobile Black Bears, and he was the last kid out of the Negro Leagues in '53;
(And after a year in the minors when Hank stepped up to the plate in the spring of '54 for the Braves, the game was changed forever.;

755 home runs! And all that lay ahead of him in 1952, a skinny kid getting his farewell picture took at the railway station

With his mouth shut tight and his hands behind his back
With his eyes on fire

So long Alabama!

18 years old and black and proud as any man under God has a right to be, $1.50 in his pocket and two changes of clothes to his name, the day he got on the train and got out of town.

And the train took off

And the blows against the Empire began.

Actual stickball with the Say Hey Kid

A million years ago when we were free & polio wasn't invented
and Joey wasn't a child who watched from a tenement window
while the rest of the kids played hopscotch & sailed on scarlet
wings & played hooky down at the wharves

& Sam polished a stolen apple & watched while the rest of us
took turns jumping off the Brooklyn Bridge — the top stoop was
a dizzying height & no I did not break my front tooth in a fight I
only dived into a manhole cover & got lost in a man-size puddle

it was our first fire plug summer camp our fresh air fund it was
a million years ago & so what if Joey only watched & hoodlums
were hiding behind barber poles in the blue ghetto heat — there
was no cop cars to avoid, life was inexhaustible & belonged to us
& you could lie about anything & get away with it —

who took the cookie from the cookie jar

the pavement smelled sweet with bazooka gum & cabbages
cooking in the upstairs hall & we played ringolevio or capture
the flag in the park or actual stickball with the Say Hey Kid, no
squeal of car brakes & it didn't matter what borough you lived in

& cap guns were excellent the streets were littered with 'play dead'
for miles around & I saw in living something more than there
actually was — the neighborhood was as big as an entire western
movie with plenty of super bang roll caps for refills (every kid
shot every other kid from here to Canarsie)

& every night we lit fires near the precinct building & the cops
thought nothing of it, in the morning you could write your name
on brick walls with big box railroad chalk & they wouldn't come
to the apartment & bother you about it

(little Joanie Brady sat in a mud-puddle sky & drew swans & ducks in the clouds, we shot 'em out of heaven 1-2-3)

it was a million years ago a friendly universe we could just pretend & didn't think about things like love or marriage or death or consequences (we took our medicine on sugar cubes in wax paper cups stayed out all day & came home satisfied)

nobody dreamed they could actually have their own yard to play in & some day little Joanie would come visiting wearing white gloves on her pretty hands (no more fists of mud no more chalk swans) & hold tea parties

but like I say it was a million years ago when even if you were a boy you could get away with dreaming impossible shit like that

Riding the Brooklyn bound

Above us pedestrians, tail lights, uber jockeys, everyone pushing each other, Jack Dempseys every one, kings of the colossus, jungle cats the real animal, got blood in their ears stalking the ring in Madison Square Garden

and we are sons of bitches ourselves riding the 'down here,' we fought in those streets for the right to call ourselves that and we'll fight for it again, down here or above ground, when the sun comes out or when the moon commences to flex its biceps, and yeah the sun floats like a butterfly, and yeah the sun collides with skyscrapers and smokestacks

but down here things are dark, so beautiful so dextrous, even when up on the street bad shit is happening it's cool down here, in the bosom of the hurlyburly hearts going boom boom boom because we are used to that we were born pushing, our mothers gave suckle to the same

check out the man in the overcoat, O that's a meek one all right with his nose in the New York Times, makes no eye contact with the tall blonde, he was raised better than that, don't let that fool you, he is biding his time, a bomb twists in his heart, a big bomb, big as a twitching tail

and we make our way, deserted together alone or blissed out, we are the city ourselves dressed in our birthday black, we punch like the universe we let others reach for the sky, fists up or palms out we ride down low in the deepest hole we like, we like it, we like it this way

how the city manages to keep these cars moving is a mystery to me they got no budget to keep this thing running

Fair exchange

It is Friday it is 6:56 a man in shirt sleeves is hauling a trash bag to the curb in front of his house and when he gets to the curb he wants that trash bag to stand up straight the way he was taught to by his dad when he was four, to stand up straight

It will make his parents proud, it will make his wife proud, and his family proud, even though it is his wife's trash, he thinks, not his (except Tuesdays and Fridays when he's responsible for it, he's okay with that)

She fills it he hauls it that's fair exchange

Sometimes I see her hand it to him at the door, she is wearing her bathrobe, *'here honey! I tied with a ribbon!'* (I can see him opening presents and blowing out candles, the table the cake his mother's big frowning face like a loving cup hovering over his head, my little man! she is tying a bowtie around his neck)

But I was talking about his wife watching at the door (and me watching from my car, because I'm often stopped at his corner of the world during the morning commute)

Who knows what's inside that bag? coffee grounds chicken bones hot dog rolls pharmaceutical product — potato skins shrimp shells corn ships in a plastic bag — life itself the very dregs of it

And who knows what's inside that house? two and a half dogs (large ones) a wide screen tv, bedroom furniture, possibly some kids — and a wife who still adores him despite everything she has learned, things he could never have hidden forever anyway

My how time flies! The light's still red and he has made it to the curb, looking straight ahead ignoring the traffic; and now he is talking to that bag of garbage, tightening the little bow that holds everything inside it — he is using his old boyish charm, it comes out naturally, he is trying to win its cooperation with his charm

Yeah his charm! it must still serve him well somewhere sometime — maybe inside that house, maybe at the office

But out at the curb at 6:56 cajoling a bag of trash? no sir! the charm wears out — the trash has a mind of its own it won't cooperate it never does what it is told

'that darling darling little clown of mine,' thinks his wife, shaking her head, *'that bag of trash really ought to show him some love!'*

How ordinary it all seems, standing at the corner of his kingdom a man asking a plastic bag of trash to behave — cajoling the trash — shrugging his shoulders like a coy little mistress, smiling the way his mother smiled when she got caught red-handed

His hands are turned outwards like a secret ballerina!

How cute he must have been as a boy and rewarded for it too -- how cute he must have stood at the side of the gym watching as the rougher boys flew past

And I want to say this: everybody has their place and dies a little bit every day — it starts in the bones and works its way out — including a man in shirt sleeves talking to a bag of trash with a wife in a bathrobe standing at the door watching him

But it's no use I can't say it; can't write about it anymore (how sad that I'm witness to this step-back in time), it is 6:56 I am stuck in traffic with all the other SUVs. You write about it, not me. I just can't right now I honestly can't. Nor do I wish to.

I don't want to know this man or take him to bed or put him to good use or love him like a child; I don't want to be mother or father to this man, I only want to see this red light turn green

Because when it comes down to it, everyone has their place, and knows it too, no matter what they are told — even the dead weight of potato skins shrimp shells and corn chips in a plastic bag knows its place

And try as you may, the dull gray truth of the matter is gravity rules, not men — and as soon as you turn your back on things, the bowtie breaks, the bag tips over, and all the happy shit come tumbling happily out

Especially at 6:56
on a Friday morning
in late October
in America

Rumble seat moon

Every night when the moon casts its long low shadow
over Long Island I remember a girl named Molly w/her
boyfriend Ted, two crazy citykids parked under the
verysame moon, sitting in the rumble seat of a 1930
Model A Ford — they have had a swell day, aces!
They are young, they are in love, you can almost
see it in their eyes — it is summer, the war hasn't
happened yet, the Depression is on but they still
have jobs — it is Labor Day & they have spent
their day off wisely — why you can almost smell it,
beach grass pitch pine sea gulls salt water taffy —
swimming, laughing, strolling on the boardwalk
— life's a clambake! In the Jones Beach parking lot
under a rumbleseat moon, after a sunny afternoon
stretched out in the glorious sand stealing kisses

Listening to jazz on a rainy bebop afternoon

Because it is the music of the Old Daddy Hipsters turning things inside out;

Because the brightness and benevolence of their blowing in the heart of a dark intolerant age releases strength of mind and soul craziness, blows JOY back into a joyless world and spirit back into the secret bloodstream of material existence;

Because strange cats were dodging raindrops and hopping from club to club in the brokenhearted streets of Chicago and KC in '50s middle America;

Because we should be dodging raindrops too;

Because the Old Daddy Hipsters were gone magic visionary creatures of a down and out age, revolutionaries, apparitions;

Because this is a down and out age too, the sad pitiful stupidity of the world is with us in all its essentialities and particulars, there is a new sinister efficiency in American society (Jack said that) to replace the old;

Because it is sheer madness to roll with it or play the game in any nation when the communion of free soul travelers is declared illegal;

Because jazz is the secret elixir for making it in a world designed to blot out joy, extinguish ecstasy;

Because the bounce is real and the music necessary;

Because solidarity with the Old Daddy Hipsters on a rainy Tuesday afternoon is exactly what is needed in any society or age designed to subdue and keep watch over us.

When Lester Young was new on the Scene

Like any ordinary night in the middle of the big Depression cruising past W 52nd a few steps ahead of the man the year was 1936, Lester Young was new on the scene, to me at least, and pouring out the door and onto the street like a saucer to a kitten, a sound that comes out of nowhere and soothes a man who is on the nut, flat broke, a sound that comes on smooth as paradise, easy as scotch and milk — and I wanted to go in but wouldn't you know, standing at the doorway like diamonds in the light of the sun itself, Missus Harrigan in a hot silk dress — so fine so perfect I could feel the hairs on the back of my neck stand up going who whoo whoo, crazy! after what that woman had put me through —

Prez had all the right moves, he was making the night turn magic, and the way she stood there sphinx-like and unawares I almost fell on my knees, behold, womanhood transformed! no longer the dame who just a couple of hours back was shaking a fist full of chicken bones in my face — shouting 'I pulled this out of the sink myself' — 'you call yourself a plumber!?' — and left the kitchen in search of some lethal instrument to beat me with, while I collected my shit and pulled up my pants — waiting for the executioner to return — 'get your sorry ass out of my house I'll fix the damn thing myself' she growled, waving a plunger over her head like a cop with a night stick

'Get your ass out, or I'll use this fucking thing on you' sd my dream woman at 8 — I took her at her word

Chelsea piers, chapel of moonlight

This half truth, darker than an olive leaf, this underside of darkness, this shotglass oilcan harbor — Chelsea Piers, chapel of moonlight, digging this, digging ALL this, a single beam of light, a copcar prowls Hudson waters we don't care, we are darker than the devil, darker than a dream, somewhat somnolescent

Sweep on out, sea/river! I'm staying right here, immediate as spit, half boy half man, sinister, sarcastic, worshipped, obeyed, teased and tormented and flattered too; this code of appearances, darkness grappling with darkness, haunted city wary of the light (I am the very extension of the self, an extinction, an eternity)

Half boy half man, runaway satyr, risen like smoke in the company of street angels, resurrected in the dangerous church of lonely adolescence — darkness, darkness, again, again — so this is the real you, your embrace, your ritual abject drowning in the holy grail of rough trade, the real you, submissive, struggling — malevolent animal, ready to strike, backstab the heart

The real ungone truth of you, pledged at the altar of the uber utopian star, at the altar of the brokedown hustle, falling brick by busted brick, spilled like a raw rotted rainbow (fog of pickup lines and fake cocktails in the post-industrial maze)

O! abandoned friends and fistfights in Chelsea, choir boy lost in the underground clusterfuck! If only time would just stand still for a second (I'm a single guttering candle, I'm a bare bulb swinging) if only time would just end!

(I am always approaching the end of time, always huddled asleep in the long low light of a subway car growling empty through the guts of Manhattan)

And yet! this impossible fumbling, let's get down to business

Your dark smile, your seductive, bewildering, smile! Brazen and shy, you remind me of myself! Incredibly fragrant, naked ruinous masked saint, your disposable glory, chaotic, fragile!

Give us this hourglass tongue of wandering plague-kisses

Give us this chalice of randomly caught raindrops, cupped in one hand

Give us this curbside paradise, outside poolhalls and under creepy stoned streetlights

Give me your hand!

This miniature confessional, all surface and punked out, this shimmering junkie madman act, this roadmap to nowhere

Ambulances are screaming down 7Th avenue again

maybe we can renegotiate
maybe we can reset the clock
maybe we can climb out the window
(I'll be waiting for you in the bushes,
whistling in the cool night air)
never mind, turn up the news
it's the plague again 24/7
every war's the same, the world
goes radioactive, there's a 650 car
pile up on the snowy interstate (the
numbers doubled overnight)
fire & rescue everywhere,
out come the brave volunteers
from their warm beds (check
the pulse on that one, bill, I'll
clear this lady here's trachea —
afterwards we can share a cigarette)

(I mean war is comradeship, death and survival practically the same)

I was in the car too, you know,
just like I was in the war (no not
THAT war) I was in the fifth battle
of Ypres, 1918, I know the smell
of urine in the trenches, and
what it means to press your ear
to a doughboy's heaving chest —
death's unhappy little rattle — and
how flimsy those uniforms they
gave us really were, tearaway
buttons, and how flimsy the lies,
lies! in those days the bastards

would tell you anything to hold
onto their power, not like now

(and what of the missing stockpiles. and what of the war
profiteers, details at 8)

but O the comradeship
O god and country
(I never gave a single
goddamn about no Kaiser
or the Vietcong)

but O her last kiss on my forehead, cold as the cold clay, the day
they sent us off to war (the Spanish flu got your grandmother,
son, that was in 1919)

and O the cool precision of aerial
bombardment (I was in the last war
too I was a bombardier with a leather
jacket and a lucky red scarf, I lit up
a cool cigarette before the big strike)

it's all fun & games, corporal — hell is for bad guys, not us

war is crushed bone & nicotine

ashes, ashes
we all fall down
(no don't give
the plot
away)

If only I could play Faure's Elegy like Lorna Breen

This poem for Lorna Breen, and the strength of her compassion and the unspoken depths of her wounds; Dr Lorna Breen age 49, chief of Emergency Medicine at New York Presbyterian-Allen, who loved playing cello and snowboarding and posted pictures of it on Facebook, who was at the center of it all,

The impossible situation come horribly true in the streets and hospitals of New York City, the Great Pandemic of 2020;

2000 inpatients piled up in every bed behind every hospital door in NYC, ambulances idling three bodies deep in the parking lot, DOA and nobody else to deal with it but those who took an oath to do so;

(the rest of us in town ordered to avoid all contact with death)

This poem for Lorna Breen, at the limits of her endurance when the virus took her, sick with it first and then she recovered just enough to go back to work, and 'she tried to do her job and it killed her' said her dad, also a doctor back in Charlottesville Virginia;

And for every doctor, every nurse and emergency worker (of course) in New York City and the world, all day and all night at the center of the storm (how to stand at the window at 7:00 and offer applause and then return to the silence of our rooms, when day after goddam day they get up out of their grim beds and throw themselves back into the thick of it);

(And yes, how to even say the words 'avoid it like the plague,' stupid! how can I ever use that cliche again!)

But most of all this poem for Lorna Breen, 49, who loved to play cello and save other people's lives;

Lorna Breen — who took her own life after saving many others, who did herself and her family proud, who stood side by side with her colleagues, no place to hide from the terrible witness, offering all the strength in her all-too-human body, in aid and comfort to the dead and the dying,

Until there just was no more to give.

Quarantine Days

Grab me my lap
top honey I want to
Google that map
of penitence you
told me about yes
let us chart a course
of survival through
all of these our wrongs
O all around us the stakes
are high (Here dwells the proud
virus insolent as Zeus all pulse &
aggravated muscularity, a panther
stalking its prey) while through
the jungle shadow of apartment
halls nobody knows what steps
to take it's leap son leap whose
neck is getting snapped today
on a street corner or in a subway
train, hiding in the winecellar
among the corks (we are the
littlefish now) ladies & gents
bottom of the foodchain
a wading bird called death
is about to pluck some of us
up & it could be me or you
(a bolt of lightning in the
sweet sweet shallows where
we have swum, undisturbed)
steady, steady, sunlight breaking
through a window curtain
the winterclouds parts, sky
is heading due north, a blue

crocus fists its way through
parking lot concrete, audacious!
(All day long in a white & purple
robe zombie Spring moves feebly
thru the empty streets) O ruins of
Babylon no intermediary or
biblical heaven between us &
the happy strangler not even
Athena Queen of the air can do
much to protect us though everything
else she touches turns to gold (O
Athena of the mad & driven
rain, O the baked clay &
mud flats beckon with
prehistoric tides) what
seas are these how
they rise they fall
mother, like horizons
yielding to the inevitable
sun (I offer no solace) —
a flock of migrating birds
crosses the Kansas
plains, they are headed
for Minnesota & the long
gone tall grass prairie — what
memory earth possesses!
& what exactly are we to earth,
sharp hooves, thundering
herds — we are the intruders,
imposter gods, sheltering in,
wondering what we got when
we traded our souls in, our holy
original animal nature for broad
commerce & civilization (& do
not forget) it is us who disturbed

the universe turned it all upside
down (yes & our mien to live
unmeasured lives & overstep
boundaries) but see how,
across Fifth Ave. a lone coyote
trots, songbirds invade
Rockefeller Plaza, all
is well, Central Park is
a gathering pool of
sullen water, raccoons
crawl out of manhole covers
& it is all a new day
for the rest of nature,
a stimulus package
for the bumblebees,
(but who is this woman
braiding her long black hair
over on other side, what nativity,
so much desire! where the riverbank
meets the sky) & in the algebra of
these quarantined days, a century
passes, unnoticed (O one more fling
at it peoples!) & well may we return
& well punished for our excesses,
& put in our place.

(A continent wide
morning song's
pouring like blue
birds out of heaven,
into the Chesapeake,
into the North Atlantic,
into the Gulf of Mexico)

I Dream of apple blossoms and young fruit

I dream of appleblossoms and young fruit, and songbirds that fall silent, and a death toll mounting, some of them six days dead and waiting on gurneys;

I dream of cop cars colliding in sunlight and rain, of ambulances in heavy wind and hail, and down by the harbor a bolt of lightning splitting the sky and an angry seagod thrusting himself out of green seawater again and again (out he comes, grinning);

I dream of seagulls scattered and innocents caught like deer in the fever's spell, and in the front garden a veil of purple and white renegades, magnolia petals falling;

And on the radio the terrible news, I hear the dead and dying all around me, 799 dead in NY State in one day alone, that was yesterday and no dream;

And the magnolia petals too radiant for words or witnessing, and the quarantined living too flush with fear and boredom of waiting to sing or to pray;

And in the aftermath of spring's unexpected squall whole clusters of flowers still clinging to the branch, trembling above the littered dead;

Sunshine and rain, little to savor, only the taste of earth mixed with rainwater;

Little to soothe the throat or tongue, this in the year of our plague April 9th, 2020, this parachute of death, as grief comes to us with no instructions, as songbirds go silent and the sly fox huddling in the low shrub;

And as there is no way to mourn or to roll back the rock; and as there is no way to ask the stars to keep their distance, or heaven to offer explanations;

And as there is no time to count the days calmly or contemplate or reason away this provocation, only to bite down hard on the bitter pill, pour fever into a cup and drink it down;

O! open up the vaults of heaven whoever you are!

Our morgues are full, we have dug all the trenches on all the islands of the world to hold them, they are just filling up too fast, even the armies of Jesus could not hold them all;

O! as heaven is residence to you and our prayers, we call upon you in heaven, whoever you are! Try to understand, help us to wheel them down the long corridor, our dead must make way for the not yet dead (to be planted where? in your funerary sky, give them temporary rest in your graves among the stars);

We ask this small thing, it is only temporary, we will come for them at some future undetermined date, that's a promise; like minerals on the moon, we will dig them up and remember them and reinter their remains according to our custom and leave you to your own transactions;

Meanwhile let them reside among you and your stars, our orchard of the dead;

To flower like renegade magnolia blossoms;
To flourish in perfect little imperfect rows;
To fall, as white appleblossoms fall in spring;

And to bear in heaven what heavy fruit they may

Yellow moon gone pink

New York Harbor, dark waters, the Great White Way is shuttered now, Fifth Avenue's a drag strip for cop cars and emergency vehicles, and a big damn moon is rising like a single daffodil over the city, hangman moon, like an innocent bird of prey

And the ships roll in
And the ships roll out

Except for one ship that's parked off shore by the Verrazano Bridge

Waiting for the all clear sign
Waiting for the gangplank to roll
And sweet release from the quarantine ship

Don't be afraid of each other or yourselves, people! The invisible invitation to die has already landed and spread across America.

Safe Harbor? No harbor is safe! Never was, never will be. Release the passengers of the good ship plague, this town has seen it all before

Small Pox Yellow Fever Black Death Spanish Flu Polio Plague — all landed here

Covid 19, same old story

The ships roll in, the ships roll out — from Liverpool Bremerhaven Wuhan Yokohama Port au Prince — cargo ships, cruise ships, tugs and tankers and barges too; cars refrigerators palm oil crude oil bananas and grapefruit and sand. And women and men — social climbers, grifters, up tight, chill; undiscovered and overrated; the talented and the decrepit and the young. And plenty of illegal whiskey.

Stowaways too, and rich Americans with private cabins and obscene spending money.

Piraeus Le Havre Denmark Italy Holland Portugal South America Spain. All the same —
And the jumbo jets, pregnant with hope and money and death, flying in over rooftops and tenement buildings, from here to Far Rockaway

And the oil refineries in New Jersey.
And the sugar refineries in Brooklyn.
And the power plants along the East River.
And the water towers and interstates.

And the hallways ringing with the ghosts of centuries, other generations of quarantine, soup in the kitchen, radiators banging and wet socks; and the crying and laughter of the ones who made it, or didn't, gathered at the table to pray

To pray and to make it and to raise All-American children and grandchildren taught to make it too.

Old men and women themselves, now, waiting at the quarantine window to live or die.

What's the news.
When's the all clear sign.

There may not be an all clear sign, brother — just a temporary end to the hostilities
And a list of the dead, hastily scrawled.

This one wrote a rock n roll anthem.
This one wrote checks to charities.
This one emptied bedpans at night.

This one filled the mouths of the poor.
This one was a priest in the Orthodox church.
This one lectured to empty rooms.
This one invested in slum buildings.
This one invested in stock futures.
This one ran thru money like a fish thru water.
This one drowned himself in a sea of movie scripts that he sent to Hollywood and they sat on shelves for years and years gathering dust.
This one was a shrink in a cheap hotel.
This one owned a villa in Spain.
This one ran a dance studio for troubled teens.

Ring out the dead, the hospital corridors are full of them. The refrigerated truck is idling in the hospital parking lot.

Stack them up, ship them out
No time for flowers or funerals
No time for family goodbyes.
Just bury them now, or spread their ashes.

We'll remember them next Spring.
Under a yellow moon gone pink,
A yellow moon rising.

Hauling coal in paradise

you demanded it of us, you shaped our tongues to it, to work it thus, this is our language we know no other, being obedient hard-working & patriotic you laid it on us, with jingles & charms, threatened denied cajoled, you & your agents, you hooked us with it, pulled us in, you caged us, delivered us wholesale, filled our nostrils with it like exotic spices, like exotic prey & for all that not much of a price for us per head, but indoctrinated, ready to serve, we the expendable, we the necessary, to make the machinery go, we the many like so much fuel for the fire,

in Kanawha valley & Allegheny hill, under the green Irish Sea, deep along the snaky Ruhr or in vast upper Silesian fields,

soft as peat or hard as anthracite, clothed in wool or animal furs, this rosary of sweat & bone, meager coin, this material religion & black cloud rising, we the servants & the submissive, backbone of a nation, we the consumed & the damned, & it was to us like a book of common prayer, the machine beckoned & we came running, & the electricity generated & the engine ran; & bellowing soot & we running too until we coughed to a halt at end of day,

used up another day of mortal toil, exhausted, set aside, we the living, drunk deep of the bitter concoction, we the living! ruined with alcohol & coke fumes, madnesses & perils of work, resistance useless, resentment a punishable offense — a ramshackle existence, turn off the hall light keep your mouth shut, maybe the cops will stop kicking down the door,

& above all the rain in autumn

& we licking our wounds & laid up in our beds looking out at the stars, dumb honest & loyal, human animals, wondering! our father who art in heaven, above all other gods brilliant & remote, & us made in your image, why have you ignored our plight, why have you abandoned us to this! the wounded in paradise, while you go about in your aztec helicopter, your vishnu aeroplane; while you go about in your celtic shades, your jahweh penthouse of steel and glass,

& we among the cobblestones on a saturday night babbling with blood & semen & false promises, poor compensation
& we who are now in the way & never really cooperative enough to suit management
& we still talking this gutter language
& we whose backs have bent to breaking

you accuse us of failing you!

this is our inheritance, this our life's pay, this shallow breathing, nothing to show for it, broke, homeless, run off, run away,

blame us, you who offered temptation & then snatched it from our hands; blame us, you who held common reward for decent service at arm's length, then stole it away

the mine was all & now the mine's done & earth with its suffering bilious breath opens up its stinking mouth to swallow us whole

& the seas rise as if there is something they could reclaim, & the howl of the hurricane & the dessicated plain, the ruined river valley & wooded hillside exploding in flame, the sheets of rain battering the gulf coast pavement the purple mountains collapsing into ashpits

& the dead & dying mounting up

no answers, no answers, it was all we were told to do, it was all we knew, and now it will all go away,

the rust of oil cans, cast aside;
the blackened lungs of women;
men of true service, cast aside;

we who once upon a time hauled coal in paradise

5000 Protestors trapped on a bridge between America and America

5000 protesters trapped on a bridge
5000 protestors, peaceful and fearless and wise,
No rioters these, nor looters or thugs, no provocateurs of any type, agency or political stripe,
American to the core, young and Whitmanic (yes I say that proudly), great in their diversity and energetic in their vision and optimism of hope,
Hanging by a thread of filament and steel between Brooklyn and Manhattan Island tonight,
By injustice provoked, and by injury to the body and soul of their nation provoked,
By their own grace provoked, and their anger over the death in Minnesota of a man named George Floyd,
Made fearless by the electricity of their cause,
Made wise by their open eyed youth, tested against the fires of injustice set once too often in a damaged land,
YOUNG! American! righteous and un-degraded — the unstained restorative power of their voices!
Insistent, sure, voices raised in curious chorale, almost unexpected (yet they will always be raised, it is in the nature of a free people to raise their voices against oppression!) raised together and made strong — rekindled the spirit of the people,
5000 protesters, young, angry, who can no longer allow injustice to hold sway,
Or allow police brutality and racism and hate, or the division of brother from brother, and sister from sister, to hold sway,
5000 protesters, because the idea of America is greater than its errors, no matter that the Great American Idea may temporarily seem abandoned,
Because the possibility of tear gas and busted heads and arrest and being hauled off bloody and proud in a police wagon is better than being silent;

5000 protesters trapped on a bridge between America and America —
America's daughters and sons, hemmed in on both sides,
By cops in armor, with shields and guns (and billy-clubs and gas masks and thousands of handcuff zip-ties) who are young themselves, and American, and must therefore give way
To 5000 protestors, cuffed tonight by stone tower and cold steel, as well as by circumstance and grim necessity,
Between heaven above and the deep damaging waters of the East River surging below

When Ruth Bader Ginsburg stood

'In questa reggia, or son mill'anni e mille,'
Turandot (Giuseppe Adami Renato Simoni)

'Ruth Bader Ginsburg loved opera and opera loved her back' sd the headline in the NYT on Sept 19 2020 the day after she died, but when RBG (all five feet one inch of her) stood before the all-male all-white (save Thurgood Marshall) Supreme Court of the United States to defend the right of an Air Force Lieutenant (female) to be bread-winner to her family (see Frontiero vs Richardson Jan 17, 1973) and earn all the benefits accruing to that position as would any of her colleagues

she didn't have
opera on her mind

summoning the combined power of Carmen Leonore Manon Lascaut & Turandot (ie all the feisty opera heroines in the book) to her mortal frame, she showed the entire world of American jurists exactly what a woman who will not be tamed is made of

the nine leading
jurists of the land were
dumbstruck

not one justice
could say a word

not even Wm
H Rehnquist, Nixon's
bigmouthed
buddy

(*'her*
head
was in
the law' sd
Brenda
Feigen, RBG's
lawpartner in
the Frontiero case w/
a helpless little
laugh, *'&*
sometimes
in the opera')

when asked to render their decision on the question: 'did a federal law, requiring different qualification criteria for male and female military spousal dependency, unconstitutionally discriminate against women thereby violating the Fifth Amendment's due process clause?' the Supreme Court of the United States answered with one word:

Yes.

what toll it took on five foot one inch Ruth Bader Ginsburg that day no one of us may know — however Feigen later admitted this: after arguing the case RBG — Brooklyn's fiercest, most notorious (& emotionally drained) woman-warrior of the day — had to be physically carried to the Washington airport for the flight back home

it was the opening salvo in a war for women's rights worthy of opera

(consider the case of Turandot, who fought to restore the power of her ancestress of millennia past, Principessa Lo-u-Ling, who had reigned over her domain *"in silence and joy, resisting the harsh domination of men'* until conquered by the Tartars) *'you princes, arriving in such glory, proudly seeking further conquest,'* declared RBG, on Jan 17, 1973, *'not in this palace! I take my revenge on you for all she suffered . . .'*

and on that note Ruth Bader Ginsburg, all five foot one inch of her, waged a war to restore the power of women in America for 47 more years

leaving a grateful nation
dumbstruck with her prowess —
speechless with praise

Two old assholes

when
this
particular
shit
ends
meet me
in the
empty
after-
noon
of a nyc
bar at
happy
hour
(rusty
nails, two-
fer 2, 4- 7 pm) &
we will fly
fly away
  like
two old
assholes —
ghosts
since
they
were
twenty —
stumbling
gratefully
into each
other's arms
(the end of

another
beautiful
day
at war
with
America)

Einstein in the park

Einstein in the park
by the green pavilion
down by the lake,
feeding peanuts
to squirrels from
a brown paper sack
while a small girl
in school uniform
watches from
the opposite
bench. She is
both envious and
shy (an old man
with the ability
to hold court
with squirrels!)
Those are two
mighty forces
to be at war
in such a small child,
thinks Einstein;
and ponders how long
they will contend
with each other, what
will be the outcome,
whether they will struggle
inside her forever, neither force
winning, long after all the nuts
are gone. The June wind
stiffen in Einstein's hair,
dances across the lake,
like the winds of war;

feeling poetic today
he contemplates folding
the empty sack into
little trapezoids
and handing it
to her — here,
little girl, a ship
to set sail upon,
sail away from
this terrible world!
Einstein, imagining
billowing white
sails, is handing
peanuts out faster
now; faster than
two squirrels
could possibly
eat them (I said
there was two but
they are actually
three now, news
gets around);
three squirrels,
one small girl
on a park bench
by the green pavilion,
and so many peanuts
they will never empty out;
an army of peanuts!
Nobody knows what to
do now; least of all Einstein;
all the peanuts anyone
has ever lived to experience,
all the peanuts in the world;
the very miracle of peanuts

itself, maddening! too
many peanuts! pouring
out of a brown paper sack
— nut by nut by ruinous
nut — into the palm of
Einstein's hand

Ache of life, sweet to the tongue

Turn magic turn, earth tastes sweetest cupped by the hand,
churned like butter, my muscles working like an eagle's gyre
(o yeah, Yeats!), bathed in the naked green swelter of sun,
apple blossom breathed in while dozing unaware, say by a
forest pool where it is good to lie in lizard darkness, one eye
open to the crack of heaven, where sunbeams snake legless
through the tree branches and I drift like scent of honeysuckle;

And you are field dust in the air, tractors humming — you are
springwater, a forcefield, pregnant with your own weight and
split like a rock and the gods leap out! and white stars! and it is
June, the rustle of field mice, tittering in the loft, scent of bread,
the broth of cattle-flesh in the thorns, bleating sheep, mown
thistle, the air clear as fresh brewed beer, the yeast of it, raw
fermentation, life hurtling at us unapologetic;

Ache of life, sweet to the tongue, ache of my love and me, green
with it! golden as honey bees buzzing in new barley!

And our children, naked to the waist, making their solemn way
down steep footpaths to the sea

Bees in the orchard, butterflies in bright pairs

O! to live in a world beyond the reach of politicians &
powder kegs, the cheap perfume of global warming
bees in the orchard, butterflies in bright pairs,
water spaniels splashing free from the leash,
grizzly cubs wrestling in tall clover, children of
Lombard Street lost in white daisies; antelope
in gaunt sunlight grazing the unstable Kalahari,
prairie dog standing sentry in sad Oklahoma;
Maasai warrior with kudu horn on hip, Inuit at
his long thread of sinew — panda in bamboo,
coyote in the vineyards; elephants, rhinos,
leopards, cheetahs, giraffes, hippos, all the
creatures of the rift — blue men of Morocco,
subsistence fisherfolk living in Youtefa Bay;
Across the planet, in every land, beyond the
reach of rifle & rail, clans indigenous & true
to the honest soil beneath their feet, true to
the full measure of god's hand over earth —
O! to live among god's creatures, yet and still,
ripe with honey, drunk with fragrance of spring.

I look to my hands and do not complain

I am like you, Walt Whitman, a vessel to the one soul, imperfect singer in which soul takes passage, mechanical! that which is called a man but a shell of the same; immortal contained in an imperiled vessel, guardian to the god-force contained within, and yet harmonious to the same;

Mantra of the brass singing bowl, of glacier and of mountain in spring, the same;
Mantra of the unbent tree at the top of a windy crest, a Douglas Fir in winter, the same;
Mantra of the day-lily in the field, subject to the most delicate summer breezes, with bowed head;

I do not sing for the lark, or answer for the slaughter of sheep where the wolf pack pass; neither do I answer for my fellow man, or their concerns; nor attempt to justify what I see or hear; why one is understood and not the other, why one is condemned and the other raised up; why one society will rise while another will crumble;

I can justify neither my own accomplishments and failures nor those of other women or men; equal to all, no more and no less under the equal sun, to any; a man of my hands, simple, not of contradictory mind; the curiosity of my hands wiser than my brain, and without ambiguity, their own poem; wondering at the mechanics of the fish that swim, and the birds that fly; wondering at the strength of the uppermost branches and the well-modulated bend of earth's horizon;

Prying, questioning, nosy, inquisitive — hands, meddlesome and the chiefest agents of my own sinew and flesh — the knots in my calves, the aching desire in my shoulders and hips, the surety in my bones;

Compared to all that the plasticity of my hands;

How they grasp a pen and guide a plow;
how they tend a wound, or comfort a child;
and worry and play; how they repair a tool,
and probe the dark flesh of hidden places;

Temples of anger and love, grief and adoration;
temples of curiosity and piety and disgust;
These two hands, like yours, Walt Whitman, like your poets to come (ie me, ie you); extraordinary, typical, astonishing creatures of the earth in articulation; independent of and therefore amicable to inheritance; built as we are of the fundamental stuff of stars and as humble, and as enduring;

And you ask it of me, Walt Whitman,
and I give it back of you, reciprocal as love —

'Leaving it to you to provide and define it,
explaining the main things from you . . .' —
I look to my hands, and do not complain

What saves a man

Talk is cheap, what saves most men from themselves is their allegiance to the tools they carry, the constancy of a drill bit in uncertain weather, the sawdust in their hair, a staple gun or a five gallon plaster bucket well-kept.

even after a long night drinking beer and smoking cigars, even after tossing more money into the void than he ought to have at the track, what saves a man are the tools he keeps in good condition;

the gleam of morning sunlight on a lubricated sawplate when all hope else has faded, the smooth action inside a miter box after a long night sleeping flat and dreamless beside a woman who's become a mystery to him now.

more than the impulse of his hands, more than the geometry of his eye, more than the sure grip on a flip knife he owns, scoring drywall, what saves a man is the care he takes for the instruments of his work;

the creed of tools he knows better than his own tongue, better than the trust he places in the sacred texts of cast, configuration, figure, form, better than his own best judgement; fitting windows snug as dusk with a well-tempered reciprocating saw;

more than a crew of men with no bad apples, more than his own body's promise — more than a worksite free from litter, debris, excess vibration, unexpected overhead movement;

even more than the rookie carpenter in a new pair of workboots etching lunch orders on a 2 x 4 with the stub end of a pencil, more than life itself or his own suspect sexuality, no wasted conversation or bitterness to distract him;

with loyalty to the tools of his trade, with confidence in their loyalty back — the faith to put full weight into honest effort, to ascend, rung by rung, to astonishing heights;

to cut and to join, to go shoulder to shoulder with framers and fabricators despite their strangenesses and limitations.

to honor the gospel of a hefty set of french curves (they can help soften the geometry of the rectilinear world) is to be a child in an empty lot honoring the innocent movement of a butterfly.

a good ladder saves a man from himself —
crosscut saws, rasps, sandwich beams,
really long screws to fit hangars with,
or a full-threaded rod.

To be a working man

Things fall
apart, hearts
& ladders,
ladders
& hearts;
the stuff
of our days,
busted up
& in need
of mending —
kettles, saws,
saddles, trellises,
marriages, govern-
ments, hammers
& spoons — the
chief content of
our estates, our
inheritance, our
purposes & our
dreams, the things
which overtake us
or else over which
we have charge,
fundamental
as thumbs
(but with
the strength
of God in
our hands
we tack them
back together,
make them

make do) —
strong twine
to bind them
bandages
to hold
them;
& so we
climb,
rung by
damaged
rung,
wise
enough,
proud
enough
lucky enough
& cautious
of our
footing
as we
go
(silence boy, do not speak too loudly as you climb)
O Lord
that we
might
call
our-
selves
purposeful;
O Lord
that we
might call
ourselves
whole

And there will be peace at the end of the world

I have seen it in sad dreams & blue cafes, tasted it in the howl of wind weeping at streetcorners & inside sandwich shops, a peace at the end of the world & I have felt it glow in the low dark secret places and in sunbright luncheonettes where working men go for 20 precious minutes of solace — & me, disappointed, disappearing along with them — beer, sandwiches, soupbowls, warm pie on cold plates — spoons in clattering coffee cups, 20 precious minutes being left the hell alone while bee-headed waitresses behind tired countertops contemplate their tips —

A peace at the end of the world, I have seen it with my own two eyes, held it in my hands & I bet you have too, at the end of the night shift, busboys piling chairs up on tables & the homeless turning back into shadows & the man with the mop walloping the floor with soapy water & the bleach in your eyes & the boss at the cash register & cook in the kitchen hanging saucepots back up on hooks like samurai —

& outside on the boulevard rich women strolling past in high-heels & furs, taking their time or racing along in pursuit of hot lovers & cold appointments (O sweet liaison!) I see them too, thru grease & mirrors, thru smoke & window glass, they are magnificent, also captives to time, they are lost artifacts & grand civilizations, going where daylight goes & everything with it, to where eternity bleeds what's black & holy back into the world & all this stupidity ends, all this! which surrounds us & fills the heart of every woman & man past all holding —

& all of us walking to the same metronome, thru sunshine & icy rain, toward the light at the end of the world, where peace begins

Look down into Lorca's grave, poet

Look down into Lorca's grave, poet,
in the dry barren wasteland between
Plot 9 and the road to Alfacar, into a
silence buried in the mean grounds
of Granada where the great springs
of Spain sang so sweet -- the butt
end of a fascist rifle took care of that
(last night wrestling in the arms of the
fever, all the same); death comes so
calm, so bright, in the end the divine
power of the pen is no match for a
blindfold and a Spanish cigarette —
they cut the rings from your hair,
sapped the strength from your hands —
they robbed the treasure out of your eyes,
Garcia Lorca, and rode away; and death
comes to us all, memory and soul, where
is the mirror I saw you disrobe in by
candlelight, where the locket you put
around my neck, in love's sorry name?
How strange, the end of days, a young man
with a songbird still caught in his throat,
wearing old men's clothes. And then this:
lingering and last departure, hanging on
at the edge of the crowd, neither terrified
nor tamed — estranged, useless, forgotten,
cheering the chattel on, no appetite left
for love or fear or wine or even bread.

About the Author

George Wallace is writer in residence at the Walt Whitman Birthplace, editor of Poetrybay, and author of 37 previous collections of poetry, including *Smashing Rock and Straight As Razors* (Blue Light Press, 2017). Based in the New York City performance scene, he teaches at Pace University in Manhattan and travels internationally to conduct readings and present his work. Recent awards and honors include: Corona d'oro (Korca Literary Festival AB) 2019; Orpheus Prize (Orpheus Festival, BG) 2018; Alexander the Great Gold Medal (UNESCO-Salamis, GR) 2018; Centro Studii Archivio d'Occidente Award (CSAO, It) 2018; Naim Frasheri Prize and Festival Laureate (Ditet e Naimit Festival, MK) 2017; Blue Light Book Award 2017; Laureate, National Beat Poetry Festival 2015-16.

Publications

Outside Paso Robles: California Poems (Amethyst & Emerald Pub, 2019)

I Feed the Flames and the Flames Feed Me (Local Gems Press, 2019)

Sacred Language of Wine and Bread (La Finestra Editrice IT, 2019)

One Hundred Years Among The Daisies (Spartan Press, 2018)

The Sulphur of Troy / Lo Zolfo di Troia (La Finestra Editrice IT, 2018)

Midnight Angels / Engjejt e Nates (Ditet e Naimit, Macedonia, 2018)

Smashing Rock And Straight As Razors (Blue Light Press, 2017)

A Simple Blues With A Few Intangibles (Foothills Publishing, 2016)

Drugged By Hollywood (NightBallet Press, 2016)

Beauty Parlors, Trainyards and Everything In Between (Spartan Press, 2014)

Belt Buckles and Bibles (NightBallet Press, 2013)

Riding With Boom Boom (NightBallet Press, 2013)

EOS: Abductor of Men (Three Rooms Press, 2012)

Incident on the Orient Express (Nirala Publications, India, 2012)

Sleeping Beauty's Revenge (NightBallet Press, 2012)

The Hard Stuff (NightBallet Press, 2012)

Jumping Over The Moon (Boone's Dock Press, 2011)

Poppin Johnny (Three Rooms Press, 2009)

Summer Of Love, Summer Of Love (Shivastan Press, 2008)

Sunny Side Up The Dream Cloud Egg (Good Japan Press, 2008)

Who's Handling Your Aubergines (Green Panda Press, 2008)

Wrestling Godzilla (Green Panda Press, 2007)

When I Was Dead (Flarestack Publishing U.K., 2006)

After The Fall (Butcher Shop Press, 2005)

50 Love Poems / 50 Poesie D'Amore (La Finestra Editrice IT, 2004)

Burn My Heart In Wet Sand (Troubadour UK, 2004)

Without Benefit Of Men (Chlenskiy Publishing, 2004)

Swimming Through Water / Nuotando Attraverso L'Aqua (La Finestra Editrice IT, 2003)

Poems of Augie Prime (Writers Ink Press, 1999)

Tales of a Yuppie Dropout (Writers Ink Press, 1992)

The Milking Jug (Cross-Cultural Communications, 1989)

Tie Back The Roses (Explicitly Graphic UK 1986)

CPSIA information can be obtained
at www.ICGtesting.com
Printed in the USA
JSHW020524210621
15946JS00002B/15